ROWLEY LEIGH

NO PLACE
LIKE HOME

ROWLEY LEIGH

NO PLACE
LIKE HOME

CLEARVIEW BOOKS

Published in the UK in 2012 by Clearview Books
11 Grosvenor Crescent, London SW1X 7EE

First published by Fourth Estate in 2000

A CIP catalogue record for this book is available
from the British Library

ISBN 978 1 908337 10 8

Cover and book design by Jojo Hastie Design

Printed in the UK by Bell & Bain Ltd., Glasgow

CONTENTS

Introduction   6

Spring   9
   Easter Sunday Lunch   12
   The Americans are Coming   19
   The Fishetarian Aunt or Ladies
      Who Lunch   24
   In Spring a Young Man's Fancy   28
   Still Courting: a Foursome   33
   Interlude: Potatoes   38

Summer   43
   The Barbecue   46
   A Classic Summer Lunch   53
   Summer Supper for Two: "The
      Incredible Lightness of Being" 59
   Picnic   65
   Alfresco Dinner   72
   Interlude: Rice   77

Autumn   83
   The Club Dinner for the
      Rich Uncle   86
   Mushroom Gatherers' Lunch   92
   Supper Party   97
   Hallowe'en Night: Tricks
      and Treats   104
   A Vegetarian Lunch   111
   Interlude: Pasta   116

Winter   121
   Dinner for Two   124
   Footballers' Lunch   131
   The Dinner Party   136
   Boxing Day Lunch   143
   The Vegetarian in Lent   150

   Glossary   155

   Index   157

INTRODUCTION

The guiding principle behind this book was my attempt to get away from some of the recent trends in cookery writing. Restaurants, which started off as the poor relations of private-house cooking, have come to dominate the scene totally with good cooking considered to be cooking as practised by chefs in professional kitchens. I love restaurants as much as anybody. I love them as one of the few ways we now socialize in public, I love the gaiety and fun of going to a restaurant and I love the frisson of gastronomic excitement when one goes to a new or a great one. I also love my job as a chef, working in a restaurant but I really do not think people should try and create them in their own home. Home cooking is a completely different sport from restaurant cooking, with a different set of rules and very different conditions.

It was for this reason that I was determined not to write a 'cheffy' book. It was important to think the recipes through from a domestic point of view in terms of timing, technique and feasibility, and to outline a *modus operandi* that would be easily understood by the domestic cook.

If I wanted to write a clear and user-friendly manual – which is what a cookery book should be, when all is said and done – by the same token, I had no intention of 'dumbing down' whatever I had to offer my readers. Far too many cookery books offer an easy way out. They stress how quick and easy a recipe is when this is rarely either true or worthwhile. Most good food takes time and care in the preparation and there is absolutely nothing wrong with that. Proper cooks enjoy cooking and, far from finding it 'stressful' and time-consuming consider it deeply therapeutic and really pleasurable. Real cooks don't want quick and easy, they want to know they have achieved something, that they have performed that wonderful alchemy whereby a bald set of ingredients becomes something quite magical. The job of the recipe writer is to describe that transmutation as clearly as possible and to take the uninitiated cook through the process in clearly delineated steps.

Celebrating difference is another crucial element of the mission statement. My litany of favourite ingredients includes the obscure not for obscurity's sake but because a world without sea kale, early forced rhubarb, morels, purple sprouting broccoli, golden beetroot, quinces, truffles, line-caught John Dory, wild strawberries and salsify – all indigenous to the British Isles – would be a poorer place. Yet these ingredients cannot survive if we do not know how to use them or have some sense of their place in the scheme of things.

I apologise for repeating in this introduction many of the themes, or rants, of the original edition of *No Place Like Home*. To an old sceptic like myself, however, little has changed, and my views are just as passionately held. Television still dominates, cooking is still too much of a spectator sport. The supermarkets – the posh ones, especially – are filled more than ever with pre-prepared meals that completely obviate the need to cook for oneself. I see no moral problem with this state of affairs, I simply think people are missing out and that the act of turning raw ingredients into delicious food is, in some strange way, an activity that is both therapeutic and helps to introduce some sense into our lives.

SPRING

EASTER SUNDAY LUNCH

THE AMERICANS ARE COMING

THE FISHETARIAN AUNT OR LADIES WHO LUNCH

IN SPRING A YOUNG MAN'S FANCY

STILL COURTING: A FOURSOME

S P R I N G

Spring provides many examples of seasonal originals that are infinitely better than their usurpers manufactured on an industrial scale. Those who say they cannot taste the difference between a wild salmon and a farmed one are unlikely to have put it to the test – there is no comparison between the two. There's an even more marked difference when one compares the exquisite taste of a sea trout with that cotton-wool mush that constitutes the farmed rainbow trout. English asparagus has a depth of flavour unmatched, to my mind, by either Spanish or Californian varieties, however fat and tender they may be. Farmers manipulate the sheep's biological clock to give us lamb all year round and yet nothing matches new-season spring lamb for tenderness or sweetness. Green calabrese or broccoli, loved by children for its innocence of flavour and by parents because they have found something green their children will eat, pales by comparison with the taste of purple sprouting broccoli, available for a mere few weeks in April.

Some foods are still purely seasonal because efforts to produce them more intensively or for a longer period have failed, or because nobody's got round to it. There's a limited demand for sea kale, for example, at the best of times. Now, I love sea kale and cook it at every opportunity but I can't say I have had much success in my efforts to inspire a more general enthusiasm for the stuff. Rhubarb tends to know its place and is certainly at its most plentiful in spring. There are two types of wild mushroom that are almost exclusive to spring, since they thrive on spring grass rather than woodland ground.

Morels appear in late March to April. I love the esculens of that mushroom's Latin name: it rightly suggests elegant succulence. Little mousserons, or fairy ring mushrooms, shoot up in May, and add a delicious scent to eggs and creamy sauces.

There is not a lot of fruit about in spring. The winter store of apples and pears is just about exhausted but there is always the fall-back of exotic fruits (admittedly imported, but why not? They grow better in exotic climes) or dried fruit such as prunes and apricots. Perhaps the reason why so many traditional pastries have Easter connotations is that there was such a dearth of fruit at the pastry cook's disposal.

Food in spring is delicate and requires a light touch. There's no need for a lot of spices, a heavy hand with sauces, or long, slow braising. Even the spring stews like navarin of lamb or blanquette of veal are relatively quick to cook. Both epitomise the point of spring food. Simple flavours must be allowed to assert themselves and an act of faith is required by the cook. To poach cubes of veal in water with scant flavouring (an onion studded with cloves, a carrot and a bouquet garni will do the trick), then thicken the juice with a little butter and flour and stew again very briefly with a few mushrooms and spring onions, would not appear to amount to much. Carelessly done, it has to be admitted it is a very drab dish. Done well, it is a triumph, and a tribute to the alchemy of which good cooks are capable. I always contend that it's the simple stuff that reveals the quality of a cook.

EASTER SUNDAY LUNCH

CREAM OF CHICKEN AND MUSHROOM SOUP

ROAST LEG OF LAMB WITH PERSILLADE

TURNIP GRATIN

PURPLE SPROUTING BROCCOLI WITH ANCHOVIES AND OLIVE OIL

RICH CHOCOLATE MOUSSE WITH COFFEE BEAN SAUCE

Serves 8

Farmers, butchers and nature conspire to give us an abundance of new season's lamb at Easter. There may be a glut but old habits die hard, and the huge appetite for lamb and its status as the favourite joint for Sunday lunch ensure that the price stays high. Somehow, lamb enjoys a kind of innocence not just in the field but at the table. This is partly religious tradition, for the Christian, the Muslim and the Jew are united in their preference for the meat of young sheep. Food scares also, barring Chernobyl, have skirted around lovable Larry, perhaps partly because he is the least intensively reared of our three major meats. The sight of a flock of sheep with their lambs still evokes a timeless notion of the countryside and there is no doubt that they enjoy a diet and a life of exercise not given to pigs and cattle.

'New-season' lamb starts to be seen in January these days but this is stuff that has been reared indoors over winter. It may be tender meat but one can't be happy with the intensive method of production. The point is, why not wait for the real spring lamb that starts at the end of March? It has been lambed down very early in relatively protected, milder lowland pastures, mostly in the South, and produces the sweetest flesh of all. The leg yields the most meat, is the most flavoursome cut and has the right sacrificial tone. A good gigot is a splendid sight at the table: one of the many joys of home cooking is the salivatory appearance of the joint before it is carved. Not only do the sight and smell of the meat get the gustatory juices flowing, they bind those who eat it as one in a kind of ritual.

Before the meat, soup. A good blender is almost a necessity here, I'm afraid. I believe a puréed soup should be smooth beyond smooth: it is part of the magic of cooking to transform and submit the constituent parts into a different but harmonious whole. It's part of the same magic to take some chicken legs, mushrooms and a bit of rice and produce something as elegant and refined as this soup.

Eggs have to feature somewhere in a celebration of rebirth and a chocolate mousse is all about eggs, about using them to enrich, thicken and lighten texture and taste. There are even more eggs in the coffee bean sauce but it only works out at about an egg per person in total, so it should not be a question of over-egging the pudding.

CREAM OF CHICKEN AND MUSHROOM SOUP

500g wild or cultivated mushrooms
2 onions
2 cloves of garlic
50g butter
4 chicken legs
Juice of 1 lemon
1 glass of white wine
3 dessertspoons rice
1.5 litres chicken stock
A sprig of thyme
125ml double cream

Wash wild mushrooms repeatedly in several changes of cold water. Dry on a cloth and then chop roughly.

Peel the onions and garlic, slice them finely and stew them very gently in the butter. When they have begun to soften, add the chicken legs and let them seal without taking any colour. Add the mushrooms, season them well, then add the lemon juice and let the mushrooms stew for ten minutes.

Add the white wine, rice, chicken stock and thyme, bring to the boil and simmer very gently for three-quarters of an hour, until the chicken is cooked.

Remove the chicken legs from the pan and cool slightly, then take the meat off the bone, discarding any sinew and gristle. Put the meat back into the soup and then put all into a blender. Blend until smooth, then, unless your blender is very powerful, pass through a fine sieve. Put the soup back into a pan and bring gently to a simmer.

Add the double cream and taste for seasoning (it will certainly need more salt and perhaps another squeeze of lemon, just to cut the richness of the cream). Serve absolutely plain.

ROAST LEG OF LAMB WITH PERSILLADE

1 leg of lamb, weighing 3–4kg
1 bunch of parsley (curly or flat-leaf)
1 bulb of garlic
A large cup of breadcrumbs, made
   from stale white bread
2 carrots
1 onion
1 stick of celery
1 heaped teaspoon
tomato purée
Chicken or lamb stock (or half a stock
   cube)
1 glass of white wine
Thyme or rosemary
Dijon mustard

The persillade gives flavour and texture to the joint. Some people make it in a

food processor but I prefer to see the golden breadcrumbs flecked with green parsley, rather than the whole turned a fluorescent green.

Rub the leg very well with salt and pepper and roast in a heavy roasting tin in an oven preheated to 240°C / Gas Mark 8 for 45 minutes or until the meat is rare (it will be cooked some more later).

While the lamb is in the oven, make the persillade. Pick the leaves from the parsley, wash them and chop finely. Althougj this is work it should be entirely pleasurable. The garlic, just two or three cloves, must also be chopped very fine: a sprinkling of salt and some heavy work with the flat of the knife will help the process along. Mix the garlic, parsley and breadcrumbs well.

Test the lamb with a skewer or meat thermometer; a thermometer should register 50–52°C and the centre of the joint should be cool but not cold when the meat is removed from the oven. Leave the meat to rest on a carving board while you make a gravy in the roasting tin. Coarsely chop the carrots, onion, celery and the remaining garlic. Pour out almost all the fat from the roasting tin, then put the tin on a medium heat and add the vegetables. Let them brown quite well, then add the tomato purée and, unless you have fresh stock, half a chicken or lamb stock cube. Deglaze with the white wine, scraping up all the caramelised juices. Cover with stock or water, add a little thyme or rosemary and simmer for ten to fifteen minutes. Pour in the juices from the joint and strain.

To finish, coat the cool meat all over with a thin smearing of mustard and then roll it very thoroughly in the breadcrumb mixture, pressing it on by hand. Put the meat back in the roasting tin in the hot oven and give it a good ten minutes. Test again with a skewer or meat thermometer: this time it should be warm at the centre (56–58°C) and the meat should have come on to a perfect, rosy medium rare. Leave to rest for five minutes before serving. Add to the gravy any more juices that have issued from the joint.

TURNIP GRATIN

900g turnips, not too big, and firm in
*   the middle*
500ml double cream
Grated nutmeg
1 clove of garlic, halved
Grated Parmesan cheese (optional)

Spring turnips have a sweet, delicate taste that complements the lamb beautifully.

A lot of people have a strong prejudice against turnips: this is the dish to convert them. If you don't tell them, they will think they are potatoes and wade in.

Unless you have two ovens, cook the gratin first, then raise the oven temperature and cook the lamb; reheat the gratin while the lamb is resting.

Peel the turnips and slice them, preferably on a mandoline, to the thickness of a pound coin. Place in a bowl (it's not necessary to wash them), add the cream and season very well with plenty of salt, milled white pepper and the merest hint of nutmeg, a spice that should be used with more parsimony than vermouth in a dry martini.

Rub an earthenware dish with the garlic, pour in the turnips and cream, cover with foil and bake for three-quarters of an hour in an oven preheated to 180°C / Gas Mark 4. The cream must cover the turnips and the oven must be gentle enough for it not to curdle. Having little or no starch, the turnips cook much faster than spuds and they must not be allowed to break up.

When the turnips are tender, remove the foil, sprinkle over some grated Parmesan if desired, and brown in a very hot oven or under the grill.

PURPLE SPROUTING BROCCOLI WITH ANCHOVIES AND OLIVE OIL

8 salted anchovy fillets
Juice of 1 lemon
50ml extra virgin olive oil
1 teaspoon crushed black pepper
750g purple sprouting broccoli

One of the first green vegetables of the year, and one of the best, purple sprouting broccoli is far superior to the ordinary stuff. The slender stalks are tender and delicate, and the anchovy dressing a revelation. There is an excellent recipe for leg of lamb studded with anchovies. On holiday with Simon Hopkinson once, I offered to introduce the dish to him for lunch that day. He, though, was a little disappointed that I had forgotten I got the recipe from his own book, *Roast Chicken and Other Stories*.

Chop the anchovies finely and then purée them in a blender (or pound them in a mortar) with the lemon juice, olive oil and black pepper. Pare away the thick stalks of the broccoli and remove any large, coarse leaves.

Bring a large pot of salted water to the boil and put in the broccoli. Bring back to the boil quickly and cook for two or three minutes, so that the stalks, although still quite firm, are tender. Drain the broccoli well and then toss in a bowl with the anchovy oil. Serve immediately.

RICH CHOCOLATE MOUSSE

200g bitter chocolate, broken up
3 tablespoons very strong coffee
4 eggs, separated
125g golden caster sugar
1 tablespoon dark rum or whisky
200g unsalted butter
A squeeze of lemon juice

It may seem a bit of a palaver beating the egg yolks and rather a lot of washing up using three different bowls, but the result is extremely light yet rich in flavour.

Place the chocolate and coffee in a bowl set over a pan of barely simmering water. Once the chocolate has melted, remove from the heat.

Put the egg yolks in a bowl with all but a tablespoon of the sugar, plus a tablespoon of water and the rum or whisky. Place over the pan of simmering water and whisk in a steady, rhythmic action until the mixture becomes thick, white and fluffy. Remove from the heat.

Return the bowl of chocolate to the simmering water. Cut the butter into very small cubes and whisk it into the chocolate. Remove from the heat and combine with the egg yolk mixture, whisking it together well.

Put the egg whites in an extremely clean bowl, together with a small pinch of salt and a squeeze of lemon. Whisk, preferably with an electric beater, until the whites form soft peaks.

Add the reserved tablespoon of sugar and continue to whisk until they form stiff peaks. Whisk a quarter of this mixture very thoroughly into the chocolate mixture and then gently fold in the remainder, taking care to blend in all the whites without losing too much volume.

Pour into a mould or bowl and refrigerate for at least four hours. Serve plain or with cream, crème fraîche, ice cream or coffee bean sauce.

COFFEE BEAN SAUCE

2 tablespoons coffee beans
500ml milk
6 egg yolks
125g caster sugar

Please try this method of flavouring with coffee: it is very simple, and gives a far better result than mucking about with instant coffee or trying to make espresso.

Put a dry frying pan on the heat. Throw in the coffee beans and toss or turn until they give off a rich aroma of roasted coffee. Remove from the heat and add to the milk in a saucepan. Bring gently to the boil, then remove from the heat and leave to stand for twenty minutes to infuse.

Whisk together the egg yolks and sugar. Bring the milk back to the boil and pour on to the egg yolk mixture, whisking continuously. Pour back into the pan and cook over a low heat, stirring and scraping everywhere with a wooden spoon. The custard will quickly thicken.

Remove from the heat immediately and pour into a jug. Strain out the coffee beans when you like: the flavour will get stronger the longer you leave them.

THERE IS AN AWFUL LOT OF GASTRONOMIC CORRECTNESS...

about how far meat should be cooked. On my first visit to Ireland, on a Groucho Club cricket tour (not the contradiction in terms you might imagine), our first night was spent at an extremely hospitable country-house restaurant. A charming lady, not young, came round and took our order. The first two asked for lamb. The next, my friend Liam Carson, who was manager of the club at the time, ordered the same, asking if he could possibly have his lamb pink. Of course, of course, concurred the hostess and continued with her orders, this time asking each tourist in turn if they would be wanting their lamb pink as well. The final order was probably two salmon and fifteen lamb, all pink. After some time, several pints of Guinness and some soup, the meat finally arrived, cooked a uniform grey throughout. By this time, no one cared to complain nor, it must be said, would we have had the ill grace to do so. The meat was devoured with relish, for it was some of the sweetest and most flavoursome any of us had tasted, however 'overcooked' it may have been.

I still prefer my lamb pink, however. For me there is a perfect point when the meat has been transformed, the tissue has been made tense by the impact of the heat and yet it is still bloody and succulent. Call it medium rare if you like. What I find unpleasant is lamb that has not been cooked to that extent. The French are past masters at serving up raw gobbets of unrested meat and pretending to enjoy it, and plenty of chefs have followed suit over here. I find the practice barbaric but then I am probably getting squeamish in my old age.

I believe cooking brings out flavour. A French bean that has been merely shown some hot water may be nutritionally correct but tastes of starch and little else. Given a few moments longer, it should still be green and have a slight crunch but the extra cooking will have removed that starch and allowed the true flavour to be released. So it is with lamb and several other meats besides, such as duck and many game birds, which have been victims of gastronomic correctness. I would rather have any of these things well done than hardly done at all.

THE AMERICANS ARE COMING

SEA KALE WITH BLOOD ORANGE HOLLANDAISE

SEA TROUT FILLET WITH A HORSERADISH CRUST

RHUBARB FOOL
Serves 6

Let us suppose we have some dinner guests from foreign parts. It could be the Yanks and it could be the French. It could be the Chinese for all it mattered, but there are times when we should show off a bit. After all, when we go to Paris we don't order a Chinese, and when in Rome we want to eat as the Romans do. Even if I go to the US I don't want to eat French food or Italian food, I want American – at least I think I do, although experience is a great teacher. Most foreigners will have some vague notions of steak and kidney pudding and roast beef with Yorkshire pudding and they will be amazed if you offer them something different. I have constructed a

menu that should bedazzle the putative foreigner who's coming to dinner.

We could do this at any time of year. In September half a dozen native oysters and a grouse would see them off, while in February some Scottish scallops and an Aberdeen Angus steak would do the job. Our indigenous storehouse of foods is a wonder that never ceases to delight, even if we don't always have a tradition of knowing what to do with it once we've got it.

Some years ago, in some strange, government-sponsored demonstration of Anglo-French concord, I was 'twinned' with a chef from Paris, a glamorous whizz who, like Prince and Nijinski, went by a single moniker, his being Yvan. He turned out to be utterly charming, and spent a couple of days in my kitchen at the restaurant. Though I say it myself, he was impressed. He was amazed by the quality of our ingredients and by the style of the food. The one thing he had to take home, that he'd never seen in his life before, was the *crambes maritimes*, or sea kale. I didn't like to tell him that 99.9 per cent of the population over here wouldn't know a stick of sea kale from a rhino horn, for it would have undermined my swelling national pride.

Sea trout is a fish of the finest flavour and an exquisite delicacy of texture. I can buy it in March and April ridiculously cheaply from a bunch of anglers in Northern Ireland, who abruptly abandon their efforts the minute eels come into season, on the grounds that they can get a much higher price (in Paris, of course) for those slippery migrants than for the noble trout. I can only conclude that the ubiquity and tastelessness of farmed trout has so traduced that fish's reputation that it has become almost impossible to sell. Every year I buy the trout in paroxysms of excitement, only to be disappointed at how few share my enthusiasm. Say not the struggle nought availeth.

With the fish, a salad perhaps, or some peas, or nothing green at all, but we must have our Jerseys. These days there is a bewildering choice of new potatoes. There are Charlottes and Rattes, Belles de Fontenay and the eccentric and delicious Pink Fir Apples, but the Jersey Royal is still king. No potato comes near

it for flavour, no other has such a firm but melting texture. The answer, as one old radio ham never tired of saying, lies in the soil. It must do. All over the island of Jersey tiny holdings are devoted to the crop. This is not entirely surprising, since the price of these peerless miniature beauties makes them the Romanée-Conti of the spud world, and their labours are almost as well rewarded.

To finish this flag-waving exercise is simple. Although the French have discovered rhubarb recently, it remains an utterly English phenomenon. Furthermore, the elegant simplicity of the method of making the fool and the balance between sweet and sour of the final taste epitomise all that is best about English food.

It would be very ambitious to try and make this meal all at the last minute. The sauce for the fish can be made an hour before the meal and the hollandaise will wait in a warm place while the sea kale cooks. Since it takes less than ten minutes to cook, do not bother to start the fish until you have enjoyed the kale at leisure.

SEA KALE WITH BLOOD ORANGE HOLLANDAISE

1kg sea kale
250g unsalted butter
4 egg yolks
Juice of 2 blood oranges
Juice of ½ lemon

I am a dedicated maker of hollandaise the old-fashioned way, with a bowl and a whisk on a gentle flame or in a bain marie. No instant recipes with blenders and raw egg yolks, which produce something more akin to a warm mayonnaise, ever come close to the real thing, to my mind.

Wash the sea kale well to remove any soil at the base. If it is not very fresh, the stems should be trimmed and the shoots dropped in ice-cold water for a while to revive them.

Melt the butter in a pan, then keep in a warm place. Whisk together the egg yolks, the juice of the blood oranges and lemon and plenty of milled pepper in a heavy-based saucepan over a low heat or in a large bowl set over a pan of simmering water. It takes a while but the mixture will first become foamy, then thicken and aerate to become a 'sabayon', which leaves a trail, or ribbon, behind itself. Whisking all the time, pour the butter in a trickle into the mass, using the milky residue at the bottom if the sauce becomes too thick. Season to taste.

To cook the kale, simply drop the stems in boiling salted water for two or three minutes and then drain. A sprinkling of sea salt, some milled pepper and melted butter would do very well.

Serve the hollandaise in individual ramekins so everyone can dip the sea kale into it.

SEA TROUT FILLET WITH A HORSERADISH CRUST

1 large (2kg) sea trout
2 shallots Butter
1 glass of white wine
A few peppercorns
A sprig of thyme
100ml double cream
Lemon juice
100g fresh horseradish
100g dry breadcrumbs
A little flour
1 egg, beaten

Grating horseradish is an unpleasant job. Trying not to grate your fingers, with your eyes full of tears, can reduce any cook to a state of ignomiry. However, the effect of its bite on a piece of juicy wild sea trout is electric, so persevere.

Have the fish filleted, skinned and the pin bones removed; keep the trimmings. Cut each fillet into three. Peel and slice the shallots, then stew them in a little butter in a small pan until soft. Chop the backbone of the trout, add it to the pan and seal in the butter. Add the white wine, peppercorns and thyme and cook very gently for ten minutes. Cover with the cream and cook for another ten minutes. Season well with salt, pepper and a squeeze of lemon juice. Strain through a fine sieve. If the sauce is too thin, simmer until slightly reduced and thickened.

Peel the horseradish, then grate it very finely (try not to cry) and mix with the dry breadcrumbs. Season the trout fillets and dredge in a little flour, shaking off any excess. Dip one side in the beaten egg and then into the breadcrumb/horseradish mixture. Fry the fillets, crumb side first, in butter for about four minutes a side. They should be very moist and slightly pink in the middle. Serve with the sauce and some Jersey Royals.

RHUBARB FOOL

750g rhubarb
1 orange
100–140g sugar
(caster or demerara), to taste
300ml double cream or Greek yoghurt

A very uncomplicated affair. The only question is one of texture. Some like it absolutely smooth, in which case the rhubarb must be puréed in a blender or passed through a sieve. I prefer a coarser mix, which means more care is needed in the cutting. Best made with delicate early forced rhubarb, which should not be peeled or it will lose its colour.

Wash the rhubarb and trim the ends before chopping it into slices 5mm thick. Place in a saucepan with a little finely grated orange rind (from half the orange, say), the juice of the orange and the sugar, holding about a quarter of the sugar back. Place on a gentle heat and simmer until the rhubarb breaks down. Stir well and taste to see if the remaining sugar is needed: it is important to keep the rhubarb slightly tart. Turn up the heat to evaporate any excess liquid and then drain the rhubarb in a sieve over a bowl. Leave to cool.

If using cream rather than yoghurt, whisk it until it starts to thicken or 'leave a ribbon' in its trail. Fold in the rhubarb very thoroughly, adding a little of the strained liquid if it is very dry. Pour into a bowl or glasses and refrigerate for at least an hour.

WHY SEA KALE HAS FALLEN FROM GRACE...

is something of a mystery to me. It is the only vegetable indigenous to the United Kingdom. This curious fact seems to count for little, although it makes an excellent quiz question. Our current neglect of it is in stark contrast to our forebears, who were mad about the stuff. Look around an old country-house kitchen garden and you may see an ancient clay forcing pot resembling an inverted urn, which stands as testimony to a craze that lasted more than a hundred years.

Sea kale was harvested in the wild for centuries. Around the Solent and other isolated parts of southern England, gatherers used to mound sand around the young shoots to keep them white and succulent before harvesting them and selling them in the markets of Bath, Oxford and London. Serious cultivation started towards the end of the eighteenth century. With typical thoroughness and enthusiasm, the Victorians developed a whole lore around the correct cultivation of the plant. Root cuttings, known as thongs, were forced by a variety of labour-intensive methods involving the use of hotbeds and cellars and much hessian and straw. Even the packing had a ritual.

I have a splendid volume entitled *The Profitable Culture of Fruit and Vegetables* written by one Thomas Smith in 1911. The early indoor forced sea kale was wrapped in blue paper, as the Belgians still pack their endives, and the later outdoor crop "tied together with raffia, four heads to a bundle. Twelve bundles are laid alternately in an unpapered returnable box . . . cabbage leaves are used to protect the top . . ." Such care in packing betrays a reverence for the product that British growers rarely manage to summon for any other crop.

Today only a tiny handful of people grow this delicious vegetable. If growing it is a forgotten art, so too is eating it. Recipes for sea kale are few and far between but then it is such a subtle, delicate vegetable and so pleasurable, like asparagus, to eat on its own with some buttery sauce that it needs little embellishment. I wonder if the French or Italians would have allowed a peculiar and noble gastronomic tradition to slip into obscurity the way we have with sea kale?

THE FISHETARIAN AUNT OR LADIES WHO LUNCH

ASPARAGUS AND MORELS

JOHN DORY WITH RHUBARB

CHOCOLATE TART WITH CRÈME FRAÎCHE

Serves 6

There is a new breed of diners. They call themselves vegetarians and yet include many strange vegetables in their diet, such as lobster and sea bass. They complain in restaurants that there are no main-course vegetarian options. Yet when one stuffs peppers with risotto or makes millefeuille of aubergines, they promptly order grilled turbot. They pretend to eat like birds – "Just a little starter for me, I'm not at all hungry," they say – and then stuff themselves with scallops and risotto before ripping into a chocolate pudding.

There's no point in arguing with them, of course. This merely fuels their persecution mania as the oppressed vegetarian. They bang on about their pariah-like status and whinge when you go to the bother of making them an omelette. "All he offered was an omelette," they say. The aforementioned peppers I've been told they "could make just as easily at home," which strikes me as an excellent idea. Don't talk to me about so-called vegetarians.

All you can do is humour them. Nod sagely when they claim to have no appetite. Admit how cruel it is to cook a lobster in boiling water. Say you really will think twice before eating foie gras again (think three times, actually, and each time with anticipatory relish).

Lie just as much as they do and you'll have a blameless time. Concede that chicken doesn't count as meat. Pretend the meal is terribly, terribly light but you couldn't resist buying the asparagus and you knew they'd love the John Dory. By the time the pudding comes, you'll have them eating out of your hands.

ASPARAGUS AND MORELS

200g fresh morel mushrooms
2 shallots
75g unsalted butter
24 thick asparagus spears
Lemon juice
A small bunch of chives

This is especially delicious with white asparagus, which is increasingly available from Europe before the English season begins. I know fresh morels are hard to get, I know they are expensive, but their flavour is incomparable.

Trim the bases of the morels, split them in half and then soak them in several changes of cold water until you are sure they contain not a trace of sand. Peel the shallots, halve them through the root and chop very finely.

Melt the butter in a saucepan and gently sweat the shallots in it until soft. The butter must not get too hot and start to fry the shallots. Add the morels, some salt and milled white pepper and let them stew gently for ten minutes.

Preferably with a swivel-type peeler, remove the stringy skin from the asparagus stalks. Bring a large pot of salted water to a rolling boil and add the loose asparagus. In four or five minutes the stalks should be tender while the tips still a brilliant green. Drain immediately and then cut the stalks in half while they are still hot.

Turn up the heat on the morels. Add a squeeze of lemon juice and then add the asparagus. Chop the chives very finely, add them to the pan and turn everything together briefly.

Check the seasoning before transferring to a serving dish and taking to the table.

JOHN DORY WITH RHUBARB

1 large shallot
100g butter
400g rhubarb
½ teaspoon freshly grated ginger or
*   ground ginger*
½ glass of white wine
1 teaspoon sugar
100ml double cream
1 lemon
Six 500g John Dory, filleted
Flour seasoned with salt and pepper
Sunflower oil
Lemon wedges, to serve

This works well with fillets of those lovely small John Dory from Devon and Cornwall, but if you are going to bring on a substitute it will have to be another firm-textured, flavoursome fish, such as sole, halibut or turbot, to stand up to the rhubarb.

Very good with frozen peas and buttery new potatoes.

Chop the shallot very finely and sweat it in 25g of the butter in a saucepan. 'String' the rhubarb, snapping off the tops and pulling back the membranes running down the stalks. Chop the stalks into 1cm sections, and add to the pot, along with the ginger, white wine, sugar and some salt and pepper.

Cook vigorously until the rhubarb collapses, then continue cooking to reduce the liquid. When it is almost dry, add the cream and simmer until reduced to a thick sauce. Add a squeeze of lemon juice and correct the seasoning.

Dredge the fish fillets in seasoned flour, shaking off any excess. Fry the fillets skin side down in a sizzling mixture of sunflower oil and the remaining butter. When the skin is crisp, turn and cook the other side.

Lift on to kitchen paper to drain, then serve with wedges of lemon and the sauce alongside or underneath.

CHOCOLATE TART WITH CRÈME FRAÎCHE

300g bitter chocolate
4 egg yolks
2 eggs
60g caster sugar
Crème fraîche, to serve
For the pastry:
65g butter
50g caster sugar
1 egg, beaten
125g plain flour

It is important not to overcook the chocolate mixture or it will dry up rather alarmingly. If it is still a bit runny, there will be absolutely no harm done.

For the pastry, cream the butter and sugar together in a food mixer or in a bowl with a wooden spoon. When they are perfectly smooth, mix in the beaten egg to form a wet paste. Sift in the flour with a pinch of salt and fold it in very gently without working the dough. Collect together into a ball, wrap in clingfilm and refrigerate for at least an hour.

Butter a 26cm loose-bottomed tart tin. Roll out the dough to fit the tin and, collecting it on the rolling pin, drop it into the tin. Push the dough well into the corners, ensuring there is a 1cm overlap all around the edge. Trim off any excess. Cover with clingfilm and chill for one hour, then line with greaseproof paper, fill with baking beans and bake in an oven preheated to 180°C / Gas Mark 4 for twenty minutes. Remove the beans and paper and cook the pastry for another five minutes, until just starting to colour.

Melt the chocolate, either in a bowl set over a pan of simmering water or in a microwave. Whisk the egg yolks, eggs and sugar together until they form a thick, white, frothy cream. Pour in the chocolate and blend to a rich, dark cream. Pour this mixture into the tart case, return to the oven and bake for twelve to fifteen minutes, by which time the mixture should be just set. This tart is best served lukewarm, with the crème fraîche or a little cream or ice cream.

STRANGE STUFF, RHUBARB

I make no apologies for using rhubarb twice in this section, since it is so adaptable, for all its sour astringency. I follow the herd in this respect, for rhubarb is something that chefs have fallen on with huge enthusiasm. I daresay cooking has always been subject to fashion – what else could have driven the great developments in plant breeding that have always occurred? There was a mania for rhubarb in the nineteenth century, when early forcing, or "champagne rhubarb", was discovered and hundreds of growers in Yorkshire got in on the act.

I hope rhubarb continues to be held in high esteem. It has the advantage of remaining a strictly seasonal phenomenon, preventing its overuse. Pity the poor parsnip, a delicious root vegetable much appreciated in February and March which is now imported from Australia even in August.

I equate rhubarb with fashion, or with following the crowd. It became a byword for waffle and bores were barracked by the simple repetition of the word. Seeing rhubarb stalks under an upturned pot, or watching the cut stalks stew with a little sugar in a pan, I am instantly reminded of that meaningless babble.

IN SPRING A YOUNG MAN'S FANCY

CRAB AND PAPAYA SALAD

SKIRT STEAK WITH SHALLOTS

BAKED TAMARILLOS WITH VANILLA ICE CREAM

Serves 2

Well, it is spring. Sex must be allowed to raise its ugly head once in a while. With the glorious, cynical, flippant and very funny exception of Norman Douglas (author of *Venus in the Kitchen*), any attempts to address the subject are usually either coy or crude.

I can well remember feeling mortified to be given a copy of Rude Food early on in my cooking career. On the coy side was the romantic dinner. I have often wondered of what this dinner was supposed to consist. We all knew about the candles, the Songs for Swinging Lovers on the stereo, the red tablecloth and napkins, the big wine glasses and all that, but what were they eating? Was it

that holy trinity of prawn cocktail, steak Diane and black forest gâteau? I rather suppose it was.

Steak certainly seems to go with sex. It's the primeval thing, I imagine. We like to think of ourselves as young lions, red-blooded, steeped in nature tooth and claw. It's true enough that lions like their steaks pretty rare and skirt steak likes to be eaten in that condition. 'Likes' is too mild a term – for all my tolerance of lamb well done, this is simply not appropriate for skirt steak. Given too long in the pan, the stuff turns from being the most juicy and flavoursome meat imaginable to strands of rope, and dry old rope at that. If you don't like your steak rare, choose another cut.

Seafood and seduction go hand in hand, so to speak. I used to think it was the tactile element, the sheer amount of hand and finger work involved in a plateau de fruits de mer that initiated a sense of sensual pleasure. That theory hardly holds up. Oysters are considered the greatest aphrodisiac of all but they involve little work: they slip down a treat. What is meant by aphrodisiac is almost as big a mystery: are they supposed to make you feel randy or stay randy for a longer time? I'm sure the thing's a nonsense. However, were I to be invited to dinner and given this little menu, I might well think my luck was in.

The last course should be very easy, as one may not be able to focus perfectly on cooking by this stage. The baked tamarillos are ridiculously simple even if the recipe was originally purloined from Pierre Wynants, of the three-star restaurant Comme Chez Soi in Brussels. A little plagiarism must be allowed in a good cause, especially for such a remarkable combination, both hot and cold and sweet and sour. A bit like some dates.

CRAB AND PAPAYA SALAD

1 papaya, quite ripe
Juice of ½ lemon
2 tomatoes, ripe, flavoursome but not
* too soft*
½ small red onion
½ red pepper
¼ teaspoon finely chopped fresh
* ginger*
½ red chilli
2 sprigs of coriander
250g white crab meat

Pairing shellfish with fruit is a dangerous, even outlandish, exercise but, given a bit of a kick with the chilli, the fleshy papaya makes a good counterpart to the crab. This is a white-meat-only recipe. Serve in the shell, if you have it.

Cut the papaya in quarters, remove the seeds and then peel off the skin with a potato peeler or a small, sharp knife. Cut the flesh into cubes no bigger than your little fingernail and place in a bowl. Pour over the lemon juice and sprinkle with a little sea salt and some coarsely milled black pepper.

Remove the cores from the tomatoes, put the tomatoes in a bowl and pour boiling water over them. Let stand for fifteen seconds, then drain, refresh with cold water and peel off the skins. Cut in half and remove the seeds with a teaspoon. Cut into dice the same size as the papaya and mix with the fruit. Peel and finely chop the red onion and add to the papaya and tomato.

Remove the seeds and white pith from the red pepper, then remove the skin with a potato peeler. Chop the pepper into very fine dice and add to the salad with the fresh ginger. Deseed the chilli and chop very finely. Proceed cautiously: add a little to the salad now and add more later to taste. Whereas you want a distinct 'kick' from the fiery capsicum, it should not be overwhelming. Wash your hands copiously when you have finished dealing with the chilli.

Pick the leaves from the coriander, wash them well and chop coarsely without bruising them too much. Add these to the papaya salad. Mix the ingredients really well and then taste for seasoning. Leave to macerate for an hour so that the flavours can meld together.

Fill the crab shell with this mixture. Check that the white meat is free of shell and then pile it up on top of the papaya salad absolutely as is, with no additional seasoning. Serve the salad with very thin, dry toast.

SKIRT STEAK WITH SHALLOTS

3 shallots
Butter
1 glass of red wine
Oil
450g skirt steak (i.e. 225g per person)

Good skirt steak is hard to find but is worth seeking out. Its one drawback in that it turns to sisal carpet when overcooked.

Peel the shallots and cut them into fine rings. Colour these in a little butter in a hot, heavy-based frying pan. When they are golden brown, add two thirds of the wine and transfer the mixture to a saucepan. Simmer slowly to reduce by half.

Wipe the frying pan dry, add a film of oil and get it very hot. Season the steaks well and cook for about two minutes on each side: they will cook quite quickly and are easily overcooked.

Transfer to a warm plate. Do not let them sit in their juices as they release them, but save them. Add the remaining wine to the hot frying pan, scrape up the juices and boil until well reduced. Add the shallot sauce, season, and pour in the juice from the steaks. Whisk a little knob of butter into the sauce, return the steaks to the pan to warm very briefly and serve immediately.

BAKED TAMARILLOS WITH VANILLA ICE CREAM

100g frozen raspberries
1 1/2 tablespoons caster sugar
A squeeze of lemon juice
Vanilla ice cream
3 tamarillos
1 dessertspoon soft brown sugar

It is usually best to keep the tamarillos for a few days first to ripen. Put the first three ingredients in a bowl and leave to macerate for twenty minutes, then push through a sieve to make a smooth raspberry sauce. Let the ice cream soften slightly at room temperature.

Cut the tamarillos in half lengthways, splitting the stalks. Place the fruit cut-side up on a baking tray and sprinkle with the soft brown sugar. Bake in an oven preheated to 230°C / Gas Mark 8 for fifteen minutes. The sugar should not caramelise but the tamarillos will puff up a little out of their skins and bubble over with sugary juices.

Place a spoonful of the raspberry sauce on each plate. Place three tamarillo halves so that they meet in the middle. Place a large spoonful of ice cream on top of the tamarillos in the centre and serve immediately.

LEARNING HOW TO COOK A STEAK TO YOUR LIKING

is the result of observation and knowing how a steak feels to the touch. There are visual clues. When it first sees the flame, the surface swells slightly before it progressively shrinks as it cooks. A rare steak, for example, will still be slightly plump and will not have started to shrink. A few beads of juice will start to appear on the surface when the steak is medium rare, which will quickly become pools of blood as the steak progresses through medium to well done. I have known nervous cooks assume that when the steak releases a lot of blood it must still be rare inside, which is the opposite of the case. It is not a good idea to cut the steak open to peer in and check doneness. For one thing, blood will gush out, thus drying out the steak; for another, the steak will always appear less cooked and seem raw in the middle before it has rested.

Whatever the appearance, touch is the supreme test. A finger placed gently on the surface of the meat can tell the cook all they need to know. As the heat increases inside the steak, the muscle stiffens and the fibres coalesce. A rare steak will still feel soft to the touch when it comes off the grill. The meat becomes progressively firmer: medium rare will present a slight resistance and by the time it is well done it will be quite hard. There are various ways of explaining these differences in feel (the cushion on the palm of your hand beneath your thumb under varying tension from the position of the thumb is the classic), but understanding what is going on inside the meat is the best guide.

If you like a steak blue, the rules are different. Steak should never be cooked straight from the fridge but with a blue steak this is even more important because of the shorter cooking time. Brought up to room temperature, it should be placed over a very high flame (a ridged grill pan is best), given just long enough – say, a minute – to form a charred crust on each side and then whipped off immediately. Since the heat never really reaches the centre (which should be warm but not hot) it will not need to rest but should be served immediately. Otherwise, I maintain it takes the same length of time to cook a steak whether you do it rare, medium or well done. This may puzzle some readers but bear with me. That a steak is better after a rest is a truism not always understood. When blasted with heat, the outer fibres are quickly seared, go dry and lose colour. The interior of

the meat is still raw. When the steak is removed from the grill and rested for a while, an interchange takes place: the heat from the outside warms up the blood in the middle, which in turn flows out and moistens the outer fibres.

There's a simple way of proving this theory. Cook a thick sirloin steak for two minutes per side on a hot grill. Remove and cut through a third of the way along the steak. You should now have a strange sandwich of well-done meat near the two surfaces and an unappetising raw slice in the middle. You will also have a lot of blood all over the place. Keep the rest of the steak in a lukewarm area for at least five minutes and then cut a third off the other end. The steak should have transformed itself. Gone is the sandwich and in its place is a lovely even rareness throughout the steak. On the other hand, a well-done steak should not be rested at all: it should be cooked to a uniform colour throughout, and merely loses heat and dries out very quickly if not eaten straight away. The formula goes something like this: rare steak, four minutes on the grill, six resting; medium, six and four; well done, ten and nothing.

STILL COURTING: A FOURSOME

RAW SALMON WITH GINGER DRESSING

ROAST DUCK WITH PEAS

WILD STRAWBERRY PUDDING
Serves 4

Supposing the first date was a success, you become an item, you become a couple. You haven't signed anything, of course, but before you know where you are you find yourself doing what you feared most: you've agreed to have dinner with another couple and you are giving a dinner party.

Dinner parties are undoubtedly a strain for most of us. Most cookbooks pretend they are not. This is because they are written by a strange breed of supercooks who plan everything in advance, cook most of the thing ahead of time and never burn anything. So here's my effort along the same lines. You can't burn or overcook the salmon since it's not cooked at all. Many

is the witty card who has commented on this dish that for twelve quid (or whatever) the chef might have bothered to cook it. Never mind, it's a stunner and a conversation piece and most of it can, as the books say, be prepared in advance.

The duck, I admit, can go wrong, just. Ideally I like my duck medium but, as I said about lamb, well done is okay by me. Nobody ever complained in a Chinese restaurant that they asked for it pink, so they've got no right complaining now. You can cook the peas well in advance, too: in fact you should, for braised peas take a good half an hour to forty minutes and don't mind hanging around.

The strawberry pudding contains gelatine and must be made the day before. There aren't many puddings that I'm prepared to make with fruit, on the grounds that most of it should be left well alone and served in its natural condition. That does not mean you cannot mix it up and make fruit salad; it just means I cannot see the point of all those complicated bavarois and soufflés if they don't taste as good as the fruit itself. This is different. The vanilla custard picks up the scent of the wild strawberries and is transformed. It also stretches them and, given their rarity and price, this is no bad thing.

RAW SALMON WITH GINGER DRESSING

1 tablespoon finely chopped garlic
2 tablespoons finely chopped fresh ginger
3 tablespoons finely chopped shallots
50ml lemon juice
150ml Japanese soy sauce
200ml sunflower oil
300–400g salmon fillet, skinned
Chopped chives

I've done this quasi-Japanese effort with tuna and mackerel as well as salmon, all with great success. Customers in the restaurant always imagine there's some great secret to the dressing. Here it is, in all its embarrassing simplicity: chop the aromatics very finely by knife, not in a food processor.

Mix the garlic, ginger and shallots with the liquids but do not try to emulsify them. Wash the salmon and remove bones, scales and skin. Cut downwards across the grain as thinly as you can (it helps to give the fish ten minutes in the freezer first to stiffen it a little – do not freeze). Lay the slices on very cold plates and spoon the dressing around. Sprinkle chopped chives on the dressing and serve with dry pumpernickel or rye bread.

ROAST DUCK WITH PEAS

A 2kg duckling
1 onion
2 carrots
2 sticks of celery
4 cloves of garlic
¼ bottle white or red wine, nothing
*   fancy*
2 sprigs of thyme
500ml chicken or duck stock, or
*   chicken stock cube and water*
1 teaspoon potato flour or cornflour,
*   dissolved in 1 dessertspoon port or*
*   water*
For the peas: 2 bunches of spring
*   onions*
1 small lettuce
400g shelled peas
1 sprig of mint
100g butter

Season the duck cavity with salt and pepper and truss the duck. Prick the skin around the thighs, back and lower breast. Dry the duck thoroughly and place it on its back in a roasting tin in an oven preheated to 220°C / Gas Mark 7 for twenty-five minutes until lightly browned. Reduce the oven to 180°C / Gas Mark 4 and turn the duck on its side.

After ten minutes, turn the duck on its other side, then after another ten minutes turn it back upright. While this is going

on, peel the onion and carrots and, along with the celery, chop them into dice of less than a centimetre. Chop the garlic cloves in half. Sprinkle the duck breast with some coarse salt and place the vegetables and garlic around it. Return to the oven for another fifteen minutes.

While the duck is cooking, prepare the peas. Peel back the outer skin of the spring onions, trim the bases and cut them into short finger lengths (reserve the tops for another use). Remove the central stalk of the lettuce and slice the leaves into very thin ribbons. Place all the ingredients in a saucepan with two tablespoons of water and a good seasoning of salt and pepper. Cover well and cook on a very moderate heat, checking from time to time to make sure there is enough liquid.

The water will be absorbed and the peas will swell up, be very tender and coated in their own liquor.

When the duck is done, discard the trussing strings and place it on a serving dish, leaving the vegetables in the roasting tin. Place the duck in the turned-off oven, leaving the door ajar.

Remove as much fat as you can from the roasting tin and put the tin on the hob. Add the wine and boil it down rapidly, scraping up the coagulated roasting juices, until it is reduced to about a glassful. Add the thyme and stock and boil until reduced by half. Whisk in the potato flour or cornflour mixture to thicken, then season, pouring any juices from the duck back into the sauce. Strain the sauce, preferably through a conical sieve.

Remove the legs from the duck and carve large slices from the thighs, parallel to the bone. Carve thin slices from the breast while still on the bone and distribute the meat on a bed of the peas, whose juices should mingle with those of the duck. Serve with quick-roast potatoes with onions, garlic and rosemary (see page 41).

WILD STRAWBERRY PUDDING

250g wild strawberries
100g strawberries
100g caster sugar
1 vanilla pod
250ml milk
3 gelatine leaves
4 egg yolks
250ml double or whipping cream

Sort through the wild strawberries, picking out any soft and mushy ones and adding them to the ordinary strawberries. Reserve all the good wild strawberries

for the pudding; purée the rest with the other strawberries and two tablespoons of the sugar to make a sauce. then strain through a sieve.

Split the vanilla pod in half, put it in a pan with the milk and bring to the boil. Remove from the heat and leave to infuse for twenty minutes. Soak the gelatine leaves in some tepid water for about ten minutes. Whisk the egg yolks and the remaining sugar together very well before pouring the milk over them in a thin stream, whisking constantly.

Pour back into the pan and return to the heat. Cook gently, stirring very well with a wooden spoon, until the mixture begins to thicken – the custard should be thick enough to coat the back of the spoon. Remove from the heat. Drain the gelatine, add it to the custard and whisk well to dissolve, then strain through a fine sieve. Leave to cool.

Whip the cream until it thickens and 'forms a ribbon'. Fold the cooled custard into the whipped cream and then add the wild strawberries, folding them, too, delicately into the mixture. Pour into a mould and chill for at least four hours, until set.

Turn the pudding out on to a pretty plate and surround with the sauce.

ROAST DUCK DISAPPEARED FROM POSH RESTAURANT MENUS...

sometime in 1976. This, at least, is my recollection. Michel Guérard, the first of the *nouvelle cuisine* chefs to get any publicity over here, did a *magret* of duck and we were off. Everybody did breast of duck with green peppercorns, with peaches, with kiwi fruit and a good deal else. It suited restaurants very well. Instead of cooking a whole bird in advance, then jointing and reheating it, they had a perfect, portion-controlled item that could be cooked to order, rare as you like and no wastage. Roast duck fell into disrepute. Duck *à l'orange*, almost as popular as steak Diane a few years earlier, became a cruel joke in a cardboard box performed by a company called Alveston Kitchens.

Nothing exemplifies the difference between restaurant cooking and home efforts more than the dear old duck. The restaurant magret can arrive at the table perfectly cooked, with an exquisite sauce and no mistakes. The home effort is a much messier proposition, especially when done properly and carved at the table. It does, however, have a sense of sacrament entirely missing from the restaurant. It also has all the tasty bits, the wings, the oysters, and others that have been carefully trimmed away by the chef. Posh restaurants used to do the thing properly, of course, but you'd have to go to France to see a few relics performing. I used to work with one such relic, who never tired of telling the story of the time he worked at the incredibly posh La Réserve at Beaulieu in the South of France, when that area was a playground for rich Brits. The young commis begged his *chef de rang* to be allowed to carve the duck on the terrace where the MacAlpines were lunching: the senior relented, and my friend attacked the duck with so much enthusiasm that it slipped off the trolley and fell into the swimming pool below.

There is one restaurant in this country that has never lost faith with duck. I'm not allowed to mention its name but I can tell you it is off the tarmac down a dirt track in a remote part of Anglesey. For thirty years it has opened only on Saturday nights and every one of those nights it has served duck *à l'orange*. I'm not allowed to mention it because they are too busy already.

INTERLUDE

POTATOES

We have many ways of taking carbohydrate and we may eat more bread or more pasta or even more rice, but, for most of us, potatoes are our first love. We never tire of chips, mash and roast potatoes, and everyone, or their mother, knows how these are best made, what varieties of potato should be used, when they should be peeled, how they should be cut, if they should be rinsed, which fat or oil should be employed and countless other details that pertain to their preparation.

BASIC MASH

1kg large maincrop potatoes
200ml milk
100–200g unsalted butter, at room
*   temperature*
Serves a hungry 4 or a modest 6

There is a lot of advice about making mash and, more specifically, how to prevent it becoming gluey. As is so often the case, timing is the key. If undercooked or overcooked, the starch in the potato will separate from the mass and turn the mash sticky. This is why it is necessary to cut large potatoes into smaller pieces, otherwise the outside would break up before the centre was cooked. 'Overworking' the potatoes after they have been cooked will also release the starch: handle with care.

Mashing spuds with an ordinary masher can only please those who actually like lumps in their mash. It gives a better result than a food processor, which turns the stuff to superglue in an instant. I am devoted to the mouli-légumes, which produces an excellent result with very little effort. Purists argue that a potato ricer or a drum sieve, used correctly, will 'work the purée less, but I am unconvinced.

Peel the potatoes and cut them into pieces about 5cm in diameter. Rinse briefly in cold water and then place in a saucepan, cover with plenty of cold water and add a generous pinch of salt. Bring to the boil then turn down to a gentle simmer (rapid boiling will overcook the outsides). Cook the potatoes until a knife will pass easily through them but they are still firm, not breaking up. Drain in a colander. Heat the milk in a separate saucepan.

Once the potatoes are dry, pass them through a mouli-légumes, a little at a time, back into the saucepan in which they were cooked. Stir them gently with a wooden spoon to dry them out a little before pouring in the milk, off the heat. Stop if the mash gets too runny. Season the potatoes with more salt and plenty of milled black pepper, then return the mash to a gentle heat while you stir in the butter. Serve as soon as possible.

VARIATIONS ON A THEME

For me, plain mash is probably the ultimate mash, and much the best thing to serve with rich stews and highly sauced dishes. If you are serving it with something quite simple, such as a piece of grilled fish or some boiled bacon, then you can start mucking about with the basic formula. Here are some possibilities:

SAFFRON AND OLIVE OIL MASH

Drop a generous pinch of saffron into the hot milk, stir well and leave to infuse for twenty minutes. Bring slowly back to the boil and then add to the mash. Enrich with extra virgin olive oil instead of butter, adding a little extra milk if the mash gets too thick. The olive oil will have a strong flavour, so caution is advised. I was quick to copy this idea from Simon Hopkinson

who devised this mash to go with a simple grilled sea bass when he was cooking at the Bibendum restaurant.

CHAMP

Similar to colcannon, but a little more delicate. Chop some spring onions, not too fine, and stew them for twenty minutes in a small saucepan of milk. Add the onions to the puréed potatoes with enough of the milk to make a smooth, light mash. Make a well in the middle of the champ and fill with melted butter. Very good with a slab of brisket or other boiled beef, or with poached chicken.

PARSLEY MASH

Chopped parsley, flat-leaf or curly, has a nice affinity with mash. Most other herbs will be too dominant. Simply add it at the same time as the butter, then serve with grilled tomatoes and lamb chops.

PURPLE MASH

The strange and obscure little potato, the Purple Congo, has black skin with marbled purple and white flesh, which goes a sensational violet colour when cooked. The mash has a rich, mealy, chestnut-like flavour that is unique. I have served it with a poached egg and slivers of Parmesan on top as a starter.

ROAST GARLIC MASH

All the rage in New York last year, so probably completely passé by now. The cooked garlic gives the mash a deep, earthy flavour that will complement a rich, winey stew of beef, lamb or game. Stand plump, whole garlic bulbs (two will be ample) on a bed of salt and brush with olive oil. Roast in a medium-hot oven for forty minutes to an hour, taking care they do not burn. Lift the bulbs out of the salt, place on their side on a chopping board and squeeze out the pulp with the back of a knife, leaving the skin behind. Stir this creamy pulp into the mash at the same time as the milk. Use less butter to enrich the mash and add a few drops of good olive oil at the end to accentuate the flavour of the garlic.

PARSNIP, JERUSALEM ARTICHOKE, CELERIAC OR SWEDE MASH

All of these roots gain body and substance from the tolerant spud. Being low in starch, they also help to alleviate the glue problem. Simply cook an equal amount of the root vegetable, cut the same size, with the potato. Although the roots will cook faster than the potato, they are more fibrous and need breaking down more to make a smooth mash.

Drain extremely well and take care to dry the mixture thoroughly in the pan before adding the milk. Another Hopkinson tip: add a teaspoon of Dijon mustard to parsnip mash to give a sharper, stronger flavour of parsnip.

ALIGOT

Possibly the best mash of all, l'aligot is a speciality of the Auvergne, in which mashed potato is enriched with extremely fresh Cantal cheese. There is a splendid restaurant in Paris, L'Ambassade d'Auvergne, which specialises in l'aligot. Matronly waitresses emerge from the kitchen with little copper pans of the stuff, working it with a wooden spatula until they can pull it some three feet out of the pan in an elastic stream. Both the flavour and the performance are sensationally good.

NEW POTATOES IN MILK

50g butter
1kg new potatoes (Pink Fir Apple or
Ratte are best until Jerseys come in)
A pinch of nutmeg
4 bay leaves
500ml milk
Serves 4–6

A variation on pommes fondantes, or "melting potatoes". New potatoes are often hard and dry when committed to such treatment: not here, for the milk helps them to swell and become incredibly tender. Other herbs and spices – paprika or rosemary, for example – can be introduced to add flavouring.

Smear the butter over the base of a heavy sauté pan. Peel the potatoes, then fit them in the pan on their sides with as few gaps as possible. Season well with salt, pepper and nutmeg, add the bay leaves and pour the milk over so that it just covers the potatoes. Cover with a butter paper or similar and put on a medium heat. The milk should slowly evaporate but the tops of the potatoes should cook in the steam. Once the potatoes are soft (after about twenty-five minutes), remove the paper and turn up the heat until the milk evaporates completely and the potatoes turn a lovely golden brown in the residual butter. Take care not to disturb the potatoes at any time. Remove from the heat and leave to rest for a good five minutes before carefully turning the potatoes over and then returning them to the heat to brown the other side. Rest again a minute or two before lifting them out of the butter and sprinkling with a pinch more salt.

QUICK ROAST POTATOES WITH ONIONS, GARLIC AND ROSEMARY

6 potatoes, weighing 150–200g each
2 bulbs of garlic
150ml good olive oil
6 small red onions
1 large sprig of rosemary
Serves 6

An improvisation of my mother's after she forgot to put some baked potatoes in the oven. It has served me well ever since.

Do not peel the potatoes but split them in half lengthways. With a small, sharp knife, criss-cross the flesh with slashes less than 1cm deep, without cutting the skin. Put the potatoes cut-side up in a roasting tray. Separate the cloves of garlic and scatter them around them. Pour the olive oil over the potatoes and place in an oven preheated to 230°C / Gas Mark 8.

Trim the bases of the onions, peel them if you wish, and slit them in half lengthways through the root. Add these to the potatoes after they have been cooking for ten minutes and distribute the rosemary in sprigs around them. Baste all the ingredients with the oil and put back in the oven to cook for another ten to fifteen minutes, or until the potatoes are golden brown and tender. Serve with roast meat.

SUMMER

THE BARBECUE

A CLASSIC SUMMER LUNCH

SUMMER SUPPER FOR TWO: 'THE INCREDIBLE LIGHTNESS OF BEING'

PICNIC

ALFRESCO DINNER

S U M M E R

True summer food is lazy food. Our appetites are different in the summer months. We don't need the sustaining soups and stews of winter or have the appetite for the rich diet available in autumn. Summer food should be light and clean, its strong flavours simply served. This more relaxed approach allows one to forget the two tyrannies of British cooking: the first prescribes that all food should be served piping hot and the second that any meat (or fish) must be accompanied by at least two vegetables. Since all food rapidly loses heat out of doors, and since the bold, simple flavours of summer food emerge when it is lukewarm or cool, we need not worry too much if the stuff doesn't burn the tongue to start with. Producing hot vegetables at the same time as hot meat and hot gravy is all part of the same *vice anglais*: even the Brits concede in summer that a bowl of

spuds or rice and a green salad or some such are ample accompaniments.

Although it is the height of our pathetically short growing season, summer is in some ways less inspiring than the rest of the year. The legumes, such as peas and broad beans, have gone, to be replaced by dwarf French beans, 'bobby' beans and lovely runner beans. Since the Kenyans, Zimbabweans and even Guatemalans got in on the act, with their ideal, year-round growing conditions and cheap labour, few commercial growers in this country have bothered to compete, and those countries' standardised versions of French beans, mangetout and sugarsnaps have tended to debase their value. Anyone who has ever grown one of these vegetables here knows that the flavour when home-grown is incomparable, but they are not easily found. More readily available are the salads, and our growers are making efforts to produce more interesting ones than the feeble standard round lettuce that used to be ubiquitous. I happen to love a really tender, milky, round lettuce but so few have any heart or body to make them worthwhile. Instead we turn to the crisper Cos, Tom Thumbs and Little Gems and green or red oakleaf.

Other vegetables present themselves for the salad bowl and I remain a devotee of the classic English summer salad, with its beetroot, radishes, spring onions and cucumber. The Cucurbitaceae (there is no less recondite word for the family that includes cucumbers, courgettes and aubergines) tend to take over in the latter half of summer, and whereas I adore firm little courgettes, which we can produce very well over here, I am afraid I can muster up little patriotism for our aubergines or

peppers, and still have trouble seeing the point of an English hothouse tomato.

Our soft fruit is the true glory of the English summer. Strawberries, cherries, raspberries, redcurrants, blackcurrants, whitecurrants, loganberries, tayberries, greengages, Victoria plums and damsons, in approximate running order, make an impressive roll call. Because of our cooler climate, their seasons are very short but this slower growing time gives the fruit a richer depth of flavour than any foreign imports. Our strawberry season may be only half as long as the Spanish or even French (although there is a second cut in some areas in late August and September) but I for one don't mind in the least: better to eat superb fruit every day for a month and enjoy the pleasure while it lasts than to put up with second best, however readily available.

THE BARBECUE

BRUSCHETTA WITH GRILLED AUBERGINES AND ROAST GARLIC PASTE

TUNA AND CHERRY TOMATO BROCHETTES WITH SALMORIGLIO

LAMB KEBABS WITH CORIANDER AND CUMIN

RED ONIONS WITH SAGE AND LEMON

GRILLED TOMATOES AND FENNEL WITH BASIL

BAGNA CAUDA SAUCE

Serves 6

Barbecues have a bad name in this country. It's not just the weather, it's the cooking: it's that strange combination of driving rain and burnt sausage that puts people off.

To be honest, it is usually the man's fault. There are blokes who would not touch a saucepan but who suddenly think they are Escoffier when they hear the word barbecue. It's not so much some boy-scout mastery of fire that really gets them going but an atavistic instinct for the days before kitchens and before women took control of what we put in our bellies. He is out in the field and dispensing the spoils of the hunt.

Spoils is the word. Or burns. It's not actually good enough to chuck everything on the grill and walk away for a refill or decide to catch up on the cricket. It's hard to think of a cooking medium that needs more constant vigilance, care and attention than a rampant barbecue. Some people like meat that is a carboniferous cinder on the outside and has vermiculite for an interior but it is a minority taste.

Another problem with men running the show is this dominance of meat on the barbie: steaks, lamb chops, hamburgers, chicken, sausages – it's all grist to the mill – proliferate while a green salad and the odd spud provide 'balance'.

The secret of good grilling lies in trusting a gentle, glowing fire to do its work. All the coals should be red and no longer releasing any black smoke: it is only at this point that any food should be entrusted to the glowing bars. It is the residual heat in the charcoal that will do the cooking, and for this reason it needs to be a decent mass to maintain the necessary temperature: it is fatal to be too parsimonious with the coals.

I love cooking whole fish on a barbecue. Whether it is mackerel or mullet, snapper or trout, no fillet will taste as succulent. The drawbacks are that it takes a while to learn when a fish is cooked; they can stick like limpets to the grill; and people moan about the bones. A glance inside the cavity of the fish, the feel of the flesh beneath the skin, and the beginning of the shrinking process are all good indicators of when to pull it away from the fire. The sticking problem is solved by a small investment in those metal clamps – rectangular, fish-shaped, whatever – that make turning a whole fish or ten pieces of chicken at the same time ridiculously simple.

The bone problem is, to coin a phrase, a more thorny issue: only education or natural curiosity will explain the simple skeletal structure of a fish and only a proper appreciation of food will teach our children that fish is not some denatured, boneless 'product' but living tissue. The

simple alternative for the barbecue cook is to make fish kebabs. Some fish, such as mackerel, tuna and salmon, are delicious when seared at a high temperature and eaten slightly undercooked; they tend to lose succulence when cooked for longer.

The great white fish, such as sea bass, monkfish and halibut, should be cooked with precision, especially when filleted. Undercooked, they are indigestible, while overcooked they become dry and tasteless. My favourite fish for the grill are small red mullet, which have a matchless flavour when simply grilled and served with lemon. Fussy eaters and those who loathe bones will detest them.

Vegetables, still mostly abhorred or ignored by the menfolk, thrive on the barbie: tomatoes, peppers, courgettes, aubergines, fennel, onions (especially red onions) and mushrooms all succumb to the char's winning embrace. Even children still reluctant to tackle vegetables will devour corn on the cob that has been cooked on the barbecue and then rolled in butter.

BRUSCHETTA WITH GRILLED AUBERGINES AND ROAST GARLIC PASTE

6 bulbs of garlic
Lemon juice
Olive oil
Aubergines, cut lengthwise into slices 1cm thick
Thyme (or marjoram)
Rustic white bread, such as pain de campagne, cut in long slices 1cm thick

In the kitchen, separate the cloves of garlic but don't peel them. Put them in a pan of cold water, bring to the boil and cook for five minutes, then drain. Thread the blanched cloves on a skewer and grill them on the barbecue, turning regularly, until they are gently browned and tender to the touch. Unthread the garlic and mash very well with the back of a knife. The skins should come away quite nicely and you can amass the pulp at one end of a chopping board. Put the pulp in a bowl and mix with a little salt, lemon juice and a thread of olive oil.

Brush the aubergine slices with olive oil and put them on the grill. Mark each side with a good crisscross pattern by turning them through ninety degrees after a couple of minutes. Cook until tender.

Season with sea salt, sprinkle with thyme (or marjoram) leaves and keep to one side. Brush the bread with olive oil and grill in the same way. Too much oil will burn; too little and you will have dry toast.

Spread the garlic paste on the bruschetta and pile the aubergines on top.

TUNA AND CHERRY TOMATO BROCHETTES WITH SALMORIGLIO

100g of fresh tuna per brochette
Cherry tomatoes
Juice of 1 lemon
Oregano (or marjoram)
Olive oil

Cut the tuna into cubes very slightly smaller than the tomatoes and thread them alternately with the tomatoes on skewers. Cook briefly on all sides on a hot grill and remove while the tuna is still moist in the middle.

In a very small bowl, whisk together the lemon juice and a good teaspoon of salt, then add chopped fresh oregano (or marjoram). Add a thin stream of olive oil, whisking well. Spoon this over the brochettes before the emulsion breaks.

LAMB KEBABS WITH CORIANDER AND CUMIN

2 teaspoons cumin seeds
2 teaspoons coriander seeds
1 bunch of coriander
1kg minced lamb
Olive oil
To serve:
5 pitta bread
1 Cos lettuce, shredded
5 tomatoes, sliced
Juice of 2 lemons
10 spring onions, coarsely sliced
20 pickled chillies

'Roast' the seeds in a dry frying pan until they release their aroma. Grind them using whatever means you have at your disposal. Chop the coriander leaves and add them to the meat with the seeds and plenty of milled pepper. Mix very well and 'work' the meat a bit so that it starts to bind. Separate into ten balls and roll these out into long, skinless sausages. Thread them on ten skewers and brush with olive oil. Salt well and grill.

Toast the pittas, split them open and fill with some shredded lettuce and a few slices of tomato. Lay two kebabs in each one, sprinkle with lemon juice and add some slices of spring onion and a few pickled chillies.

RED ONIONS WITH SAGE AND LEMON

6 cloves of garlic
1 bunch of sage
6 red onions
2 lemons
200ml olive oil
100ml balsamic vinegar

Red onions seem to have an affinity with grilled meat. Try them grilled and tossed in vinegar, sea salt and olive oil, or give yourself a break and make this salad beforehand.

Peel the garlic and chop it finely. Strip off the sage leaves from the stalks, wash them and chop finely in turn. Peel the onions and quarter them through the root. Put them in a pot of boiling water for four to five minutes, until they soften a little. Drain and season with a teaspoon of sea salt and half a teaspoon of milled pepper. Grate the zest of the lemons over the onions and then squeeze over the juice.

Heat the olive oil in a frying pan and add the garlic. Follow this quickly with the sage, let it cook for less than a minute and then pour the mixture over the onions. Mix briefly, add the balsamic vinegar and leave to macerate for an hour before serving.

GRILLED TOMATOES AND FENNEL WITH BASIL

4 fennel bulbs
4 tablespoons olive oil
1kg ripe tomatoes
1 bunch of basil
1 dessertspoon white wine vinegar
Extra virgin olive oil

This should be made on the barbie before cooking the meat, fish or vegetables. The flavours will macerate together well as it cools.

Trim the bases of the fennel and remove the green fronds at the top, reserving them for later. Cut the fennel lengthways away from the root in slices slightly less than a centimetre thick. Brush these with some of the oil and place on a cool part of the grill. Make a good crisscross mark by turning them through ninety degrees after a couple of minutes, then turn them over and repeat on the other side. Cook them gently and on no account allow them to burn. Place in a serving dish when they are cooked: they should still be slightly firm to the bite but very succulent.

Cut the tomatoes in half crossways. Brush with a little olive oil and place cut-side down on the grill. Leave them until they are charred, then turn. Let the skin side char in turn and then transfer them to a plate. Lift off the charred skins and mix the tomatoes with the fennel.

Strip the basil leaves from the stalks and wash them, then roll them like a cigar and slice very finely. Sprinkle them over the assembly, together with a teaspoon of sea salt and a good milling of black pepper. Sprinkle with the vinegar and turn the fennel and tomatoes over gently to mix the seasoning, then pour over a generous quantity of really good extra virgin olive oil.

BAGNA CAUDA SAUCE

3 medium shallots
4 cloves of garlic
12 anchovy fillets
50ml red wine vinegar
1 teaspoon lemon juice
½ teaspoon salt
¼ teaspoon milled black pepper
150ml virgin olive oil
100ml double cream
*Shavings of Parmesan or pecorino
   cheese, to serve*

A beautiful, unctuous emollient for grilled vegetables.

Peel and chop the shallots and garlic. Blend them in a liquidiser with all the remaining ingredients except the cream and cheese. Stir in the cream. Serve poured over grilled peppers, fennel, courgettes, tomatoes and aubergines and sprinkle with shavings of Parmesan or pecorino cheese.

SHISH KEBAB MARINADE

2 onions
6 cloves of garlic
200ml olive oil
1 tablespoon paprika
2 teaspoons ground cumin
½ teaspoon crushed dried chillies
½ teaspoon milled pepper
1 tablespoon fresh thyme
4 tablespoons chopped parsley
2 tablespoons chopped mint

Cut a leg of lamb into large cubes (3cm) and marinate overnight in the mixture.

Peel and roughly chop the onions and garlic. Purée them in a liquidiser with the olive oil, then blend in the spices and thyme. Stir in the chopped herbs.

DOES A MARINADE TENDERISE MEAT?

This is a contentious issue. Harold McGee, the foodies' boffin (author of *On Food and Cooking: The Science and Lore of the Kitchen*, 1984), maintains that some plant enzymes and acid marinades break down the proteins on the surface of the meat but have little impact on the interior.

I can't agree. I'm convinced that a penetrative acid marinade affects the whole texture of the meat, especially when allowed to act overnight. I cross-examined a matchless grill cook, David Eyre, when he was chef at the Eagle, which is the pioneer of the new wave of foodie pubs in London: could a marinade tenderise meat? At first he was negative and even agreed with the prof that marinated meat could have a mushy texture near the surface and remain unchanged inside. How come his lamb kebabs, made with large cubes cut from the leg, were so incredibly tender, then? Ah well, an acid marinade would make a difference, he conceded. It transpired that he used the Middle Eastern trick of puréeing the onion (onions feature big in marinades) before adding it to his aromatic lamb marinade. David was emphatic that salt had no place in such a mixture as it would toughen the meat and draw out its moisture. The shish kebab marinade on page 51 operates on the same principle and is proof positive that an overnight dunking in a marinade can make quite tough meat extremely toothsome.

David had already given me a beautifully simple recipe to emphasise that a marinade is as much about flavour as anything else is. He pounds fennel seeds with chopped garlic, adds chopped parsley and then makes a paste with the addition of some olive oil. He rubs this into incisions in pork and poultry half an hour before cooking.

After all, most food for the grill doesn't actually need tenderising. Steaks, lamb and pork chops, chicken, fish of any description, any vegetable you care to name – these are, or should be, tender enough, but they all benefit from a little attention in the flavouring department, just as they need turning on the grill from time to time.

A problem with these marinades, of course, is that the finely chopped garlic and rosemary in which you have lovingly bathed your meat or fish simply burn into little black flecks after a bare minute of the grill's fiery embrace. The incision method gets around this, and it's a good idea to save half the marinade to baste the fish or meat when it has almost finished cooking. This combined attack works especially well with whole fish and joints of chicken, assuring a succulent result.

A CLASSIC SUMMER LUNCH

SALADE NIÇOISE

BREAST OF VEAL WITH PORK, SPINACH AND GARLIC STUFFING

SAUTERNES AND OLIVE OIL CAKE WITH RED FRUIT SALAD

Serves 6

To those of us who know no finer word in the English language, lunch is much more than a meal. Those of us who take the thing seriously have had to fight for our rights in the last few years. The first sacrilege came with the notion of the 'working lunch', during which people tried to impress each other with clipboards and statistics while ignoring what they ate. Worse was to come: 'Lunch is for wimps,' famously proclaimed Michael Douglas as Gordon Gecko in the film 'Wall Street'.

Yuppies may have come and gone but their legacy endures. Lunch in America is a peremptory occasion and to order a glass of wine at lunch in New York or Los Angeles is to propel oneself into one of the Bateman cartoons, those enduring images of social gaffes and ineptitude.

The point about a proper lunch is that it is sybaritic. Lunch is a great luxury. You can't work after it, or shouldn't for a while, at any rate. Lunch is a suspension of time and an opportunity for pure pleasure. Dinner does not have this untrammelled quality, for it is squeezed into a space between work and sleep, while lunch lingers on out of time.

It's probably because of the climate that they manage these things better in southern Europe. Siesta time is not just to avoid working in the heat of the early afternoon; it is for sleeping off a proper two-hour lunch before resuming work. We, with our northern Protestant work ethic, go back to work straight after lunch, but how much do we achieve? Who would not agree that they get twice as much done in the morning as in the afternoon? This truth had even been realised at my school: six lessons in the morning, three in the afternoon, and those only three times a week. Can't say much for the lunch, though.

Nothing could be more leisurely than this salade Niçoise. With no cooking involved, it almost demands to be made lazily, on a hot day and with ripe, richly scented tomatoes. It will not be eaten quickly either but chomped lazily with some crusty bread in attendance. The Breast of veal is a good, solid bourgeois dish and gives pleasure to the cook as well as to the diners, who will appreciate its immensely satisfying depth of flavour. The Sauternes and olive oil cake sounds heavy but is as light as a feather and a gentle foil to summer berries. Nothing here is heavy or overstated, but this is a proper lunch.

SALADE NIÇOISE

1 cup of podded broad beans
6 large tomatoes
1 green and 1 red pepper
1 cucumber
12 radishes
2 spring onions
6 hard-boiled eggs
1 clove of garlic
12 anchovy fillets
1 tablespoon black olives
10 basil leaves, torn in half
1 dessertspoon red wine vinegar
At least 2 tablespoons very good extra virgin olive oil

Our English style of salade Niçoise, with potatoes, beans and tuna, is a meal in itself. This is much more of a salad, and a perfectly feasible starter. It is also a riot of colour.

Blanch the broad beans, then drain well and peel off the thin skins. Skin the tomatoes and slice them. Seed the peppers and cut them into thin rings. Peel and slice the cucumber. Thinly slice the radishes and spring onions. Peel and slice the hardboiled eggs.

Cut the garlic in half and rub a large wooden salad bowl very well with it. Place the tomatoes, overlapping each other, in concentric rings on the bottom of the bowl. Proceed to layer the salad ingredients in similar rings, scattering the smaller ingredients across the surface. Season the whole with sea salt and coarsely milled black pepper, then sprinkle with the red wine vinegar. Coat the salad with the olive oil. Take it to the table in all its glory and then turn and toss it very thoroughly before serving.

BREAST OF VEAL WITH PORK, SPINACH AND GARLIC STUFFING

750g pork belly
½ bottle of white wine
Nutmeg
Thyme
2kg breast of veal
Olive oil
1kg spinach
3 onions
8 cloves of garlic
1 egg and 1 egg yolk
2 carrots
1 stick of celery
1 bay leaf

I have stipulated pork belly here in the hope that home cooks will assay their own sausage meat. Obviously, it is perfectly easy to cheat and buy it in. If you do, try to get a genuinely meaty type of sausage such as the Italian luganega or the French Toulouse type. If you have no mincer or mincing attachment to a food mixer, the butcher should be happy to do the mincing for you. I can't recommend a food processor for the task.

Remove the bones and rind from the pork belly and cut it into strips. Put it in a bowl with a glass of the white wine and season with a little nutmeg, some thyme and salt and pepper. Remove the bones from the breast of veal, or ask your butcher to do it for you. Lay out the meat on a board and trim until you have a square 'apron' about 15 x 30cm. Put the trimmings in the bowl with the pork. Rub a little pepper and thyme into the veal along with a little oil, cover well and refrigerate. Leave both meats to marinate overnight.

The next day, wash the spinach, discarding any tough stalks, and drop it into copious quantities of boiling water. Blanch very briefly, drain and then plunge it into a sinkful of cold water. Drain again and squeeze out any remaining water. Chop the spinach coarsely with a large knife.

Chop two of the onions finely and sweat them on a low heat in a good tablespoon of olive oil. Chop the garlic very finely and add to the pan. Before the garlic or onions start to colour, throw in the blanched spinach and stew gently until any remaining liquid has evaporated and the spinach is tender. Remove from the heat and leave to cool completely.

Take the marinated pork from the fridge and mince it once through a medium blade of the mincer. Mix it very well with the cold spinach mixture, plus the egg and egg yolk. Fry a little piece of this stuffing and check the seasoning.

Lay out the apron of veal, season lightly and put the stuffing on top, leaving a good border (3cm) all the way round. Collect the long border in both hands and roll it up away from you into a sausage shape. Without too much force, tie the joint with string at regular intervals so that it will not come apart in the cooking.

Brown the joint in a little olive oil in a roasting tin for a few minutes and then put it in an oven preheated to 180°C / Gas Mark 4 for twenty minutes. Coarsely chop the carrots, celery and the remaining onion, put them around the joint and let these brown for ten minutes. Add the remaining white wine, some thyme and the bay leaf and turn down the oven to 150°C / Gas Mark 2. Let the meat braise for a further hour, turning it once or twice in the process. If the juices get too dry, don't be afraid to add a little water to keep it moist.

Remove the joint from the oven and let it rest while you strain off the sauce. It should need little adjustment but be an unctuous and delicious gravy. Simply slice the meat thickly and serve with this juice and some creamy mashed potatoes. Some tender young carrots would be the perfect accompaniment.

SAUTERNES AND OLIVE OIL CAKE WITH RED FRUIT SALAD

5 egg yolks
150g caster sugar
Finely grated zest of 2 lemons and 2 oranges
100ml extra virgin olive oil
125ml Sauternes
125g plain flour
7 egg whites
Cream, crème fraîche or mascarpone cheese, to serve

For the red fruit salad:

Raspberries, halved strawberries and a few redcurrants
1 teaspoon caster sugar

The Sauternes here should not be great, but it must have a decent weight and concentration to it. A rich Muscat is a good substitute.

Beat the egg yolks with half the sugar until

pale and thick, then beat in the grated zest. Beat in the olive oil and then the Sauternes. Sift the flour with a quarter of a teaspoon of salt and beat it into the egg mixture just until combined. In a separate bowl, beat the egg whites, slowly adding the rest of the sugar, until they hold soft peaks. Fold in the yolk mixture thoroughly.

Pour into a buttered and floured 20cm springform cake tin and bake evenly (a fan-assisted oven is a help) for twenty minutes in an oven preheated to 180°C / Gas Mark 4. Lower the oven temperature to 150°C / Gas Mark 2 and bake for another twenty minutes. Then turn off the oven, cover the top of the cake with a round of buttered baking parchment, and leave it in the oven for ten minutes. Remove from the oven and cool in the tin on a rack, then turn out. Well-wrapped in foil, it will keep for a couple of days.

Toss the fruit with the sugar. Serve the cake with the red fruit salad and some cream, crème fraîche or mascarpone cheese.

WHERE DID IT COME FROM, OUR SALADE NIÇOISE?

Not Nice, that's for sure. The one-time mayor of Nice and, later, fugitive from justice (some little difficulty with the police), Jacques Médecin, wrote an excellent, if highly coloured, account of the local cuisine, in which he railed vehemently against the inclusion of any cooked vegetables in la vraie salade Niçoise. He ought to know; his family practically owned the place for fifty years. Somehow, over the years, our bogus notions of the salad have taken root and supplanted the original and it would be inconceivable these days to have the dish without a few potatoes, some green beans and some tuna.

Some time in the Fifties and Sixties, a whole notion of French food arose and a canon was created that really had little to do with it. We fell in love not so much with France but with a quite independent myth, interpreted and sold by a number of gurus, foremost of whom was the great Elizabeth David.

People such as Terence Conran, through his Habitat chain, and Robert Carrier dispensed, and profited from this mythical terrain. It is not that they did not derive their ideas from the French, just that we

learnt as much through their creative mediation as from the real thing.

For all our love of French food, we remain profoundly British as cooks. We have, after all, been copying the French for centuries. Even if we had the infrastructure of artisanal craft that forms the backbone of French cooking, whether it be the poultryman, the charcutier, the cheesemaker or maraîcher, we would always have a more emphatic and robust attitude to flavouring and seasoning and continue to rummage like magpies for exotic titbits of cuisines further afield. That is what makes our food so original.

SUMMER SUPPER FOR TWO: 'THE INCREDIBLE LIGHTNESS OF BEING'

CHILLED AVOCADO AND ALMOND SOUP

RED MULLET, AUBERGINE AND POTATO SANDWICH

RASPBERRY GRATIN

Serves 6

Lightness is all, sometimes. Some years ago I used to cook for a (very) rich family at weekends. It was hard work and I resented the loss of my time but I enjoyed the chance to cook. I once made salmon quenelles that were, frankly, a disaster. I had put too much cream in the mixture. You add it to make a smoother, more homogeneous mousse. The salmon had probably been too fatty, whatever, but the protein could hardly support the structure. As I poached the quenelles they barely held their shape, spreading out across the poaching liquid. Bits broke away and floated off. I managed to lift the bits out of the wreckage and manoeuvre them, wobbling more than any jelly, on to a silver tray. I poured a sorrel sauce (yes, more cream) over them, sent them out and prayed. I dreaded seeing the hostess after the meal, fearing the worst. "Those quenelles," she started, and I tried to interrupt but she was in no mood to listen to dissent, "those quenelles were the lightest, most beautiful quenelles any of us have ever tasted." I gasped but kept silent. You learn a thing or two in any job.

This meal is light, as befits a summer supper. It is not, however, insubstantial. Lightness is often an illusion brought about mostly by a lot of hard labour and by stretching and refining ingredients.

The chilled soup is hardly low in calories, but coming as a smooth, subtle purée it seems lighter than it is. Red mullet is the perfect summer fish. Although rich in flavour, it has a delicate flesh that separates into delicious, meaty little flakes. Because of its oil content and exquisite taste, I prefer not to swamp it in a rich sauce. This dish may be a stack of fish and potatoes but it is clean, flavoursome and distinctly moreish.

The raspberry gratin I had in an excellent seaside hotel at Audierne, in western Brittany. For once, the maître d's ecstatic and poetic description was not inaccurate. I set about copying it the minute I got home. It's no more than a soufflé mixture poured on to a plate and cooked quickly under a hot grill, yet it has none of the anxiety of soufflé making. It is just as light and it does not collapse upon itself after a couple of mouthfuls.

CHILLED AVOCADO AND ALMOND SOUP

1 lemon
2 ripe avocados
500ml milk
1 clove of garlic, peeled
100g blanched almonds
3 egg yolks
25ml double cream
1 small red chilli
15g flaked almonds

This is a kind of gazpacho-blanco-goes-to-Mexico. It comes out very thick and should be scooped out with tortillas, or tortilla chips where I come from. It will need thinning down with a little more milk if you want a soupier consistency.

Finely grate the zest from the lemon. Halve the avocados, remove the stones and scoop out all the flesh into a blender or food processor. Squeeze the juice of the lemon on to the avocado and blend to a completely smooth purée. Put in a mixing bowl, cover the surface with clingfilm and refrigerate.

Bring the milk, garlic and blanched almonds to the boil and simmer very gently for fifteen minutes. Pour into the blender and mix in turn to a fine purée. Return to the pan and bring back to the boil, then season with salt and pepper.

Put the egg yolks and cream into a bowl, season well with salt and pepper and mix thoroughly. Pour in the milk mixture very gently, whisking constantly. Return the mixture to the pan and, over a very gentle heat, stir the mixture as though cooking a custard. As soon as it starts to thicken very slightly, pour into a bowl. Leave to cool.

Halve the chilli with a sharp knife and remove the seeds and stalk. Chop the chilli very finely. Toast the flaked almonds under a grill, watching them carefully so they don't burn.

When the almond custard is quite cold, fold it into the avocado purée. The mixture should be thick but may be overly so, in which case it can be diluted with milk or water.

Serve in well-chilled bowls. Sprinkle a few toasted almonds, some grated lemon zest and a little chopped chilli over each one.

RED MULLET, AUBERGINE AND POTATO SANDWICH

350g long, floury maincrop potatoes
Olive oil
2 long aubergines
2 red mullet, 350 – 400g each
(or twice as many, half the
size), filleted
Flour
Basil leaves
Lemon wedges, to serve

Alastair Little claims that after eating this he had it on his own menu within twelve hours. We have always raided each other's inspirations from time to time and regard it as the highest compliment.

Wash the potatoes but don't peel them. Cover with cold, salted water, bring to the boil and simmer for twenty minutes. They should be still firm and slightly undercooked.

Drain and leave to cool, then cut lengthways into slices half a centimetre thick. Line a baking sheet with foil, brush with olive oil and lay out the potato slices on it. Season them and brush with more oil, then bake in an oven preheated to 200°C / Gas Mark 6 until golden brown and crisp. Salt lightly again and keep warm.

Take a thin shaving of skin off opposing sides of the aubergines and cut lengthways in slices 1cm thick. Brush these with plenty of olive oil and put under a hot grill. When they are well coloured, turn and grill the other side, making sure they are well basted. They should be crisp outside and creamy within. Season with salt and pepper.

Dredge the boned mullet fillets in a little flour, patting off any excess, and then fry them skin-side down in a little olive oil. Give them a little shake to stop them sticking and turn them after one minute. Take them out, still half-cooked, and drain on kitchen paper.

To make the 'sandwiches', put two slices of potato on an ovenproof dish. Place a layer of aubergines on top of each. Place two leaves of basil on each aubergine and lay half the red mullet fillets on these. Repeat the process with another layer of each, finishing with a layer of potato. Keep the whole thing stable by spearing it with a cocktail stick at each end.

The sandwiches can be left for an hour or baked directly. They will take fifteen to twenty minutes to bake at 200°C / Gas Mark 6, depending on the thickness of the fish and whether they are starting from cold.

Lift carefully on to plates and serve with plenty of lemon wedges and a small jug of olive oil.

RASPBERRY GRATIN

1 vanilla pod
500ml milk
6 egg yolks
150g caster sugar
75g plain flour
A little icing sugar
1 tablespoon framboise eau de vie
8 egg whites
Lemon juice
2 small punnets of raspberries

This recipe makes rather a lot of pastry cream but it would be difficult to make less. Either make the gratin many times or use the pastry cream as a filling for cakes and pastries or as a base for a trifle. The framboise eau de vie is tricky to get: if you cannot find it, do not use framboise liqueur, which is heavy and rather sickly, but substitute Grand Marnier or some other orange-based liqueur.

The gratin is a seductive dish and therefore ideal for two. Besides, you can only get two plates under most grills I know.

Split the vanilla pod open, put it in a saucepan with the milk and bring gently to the boil. Whisk the egg yolks with half the sugar until they pale and increase a little in volume.

Add the flour and mix to a smooth paste. Pour the boiling milk on to this mixture, whisk it well and return to the pan. Bring gently back to the boil, stirring constantly and making sure none is catching in the corners of the pan.

Turn down the heat and continue stirring for three to four minutes. You should now have a thick, rich and lump-free custard. Pour it into a bowl, sprinkle with icing sugar and then cover the surface with clingfilm (unless you have that strange, but not unusual, predilection for custard skin). Leave to cool.

Place 4 tablespoons of the mixture in a bowl and add the eau de vie. Whisk together well to make a smooth paste. Put the egg whites in an electric mixer (or large mixing bowl if whisking by hand) and add a tiny pinch of salt and a small squeeze of lemon.

Whisk the egg whites, adding a little of the remaining sugar at a time. When they form peaks you should have used half the sugar and should then fold in the remaining sugar to end up with a glossy meringue. Spoon a small amount of this into the custard mixture and whisk together to a smooth cream. Then add all the rest of the meringue at once and fold in carefully with a spatula, trying to not knock too much air out as you do so.

Spoon the mixture on to two large plates and smooth over with the spatula. Push the raspberries headside up in to the mixture until it is evenly dotted with the fruit. Put the plates under a hot grill and wait until the gratins puff up and brown nicely. The mixture should not move when you give the plate a little shake. Devour immediately.

I LIKE MY FISH ON THE BONE...

but I've given up trying to get people to agree with me. Mention red mullet to people and they say, "But it's an awfully bony fish, isn't it?" There's no point explaining that it's a perfectly simple skeletal structure, the bones are easily avoided and that it's worth it because they have so much more flavour when cooked on the bone. Even less point in descending into paroxysms of anger because we inhabit a spoon-fed culture where we neither want nor need to know what we eat but are content to ingest passively whatever is put in front of us, just as long as it comes in an easily managed form. No point at all.

I've been a member of the Angry Brigade where red mullet are concerned ever since I was an impoverished hippie in Greece and watched with increasing envy and ire as two spoilt American boys were given mullet (which cost twenty times as much as the sardines I lived on) and pushed it around their plates as they whinged about the bones. I've calmed down since then and learnt to cook. I still like my fish on the bone but I've learnt that the other point of view has its merits. It would be a terrible mess picking the bones out of the sandwich, after all.

To fry little fish, such as sprats, anchovies, sardines and small red mullet, make sure they are scaled and gutted. Sprinkle the fish inside and out with sea salt and leave for twenty minutes. Heat a deep frying pan containing at least a centimetre of cheap olive oil. Wipe the fish dry with kitchen paper and then roll them in plain flour. When the oil is hot but not smoking, slide in the fish. Do not overcrowd them and make sure the underneath is really crisp before turning them. Once they are crisp on both sides, lift out the fish with a skimmer or slotted spoon and drain on kitchen paper. Sprinkle with a pinch of fine salt and serve with wedges of lemon.

Very small fish, which can be eaten bones and all, should be cooked really well, but bigger fish should be kept moist, with the fillets lifting easily away from the bones.

PICNIC

PIEDMONTESE PEPPERS

ROAST CHICKEN WITH TARRAGON

TIAN OF TOMATOES AND AUBERGINES

SUMMER PUDDING
Serves 4

There are difficulties with picnics in this country. What we think of as the long, hazy days of summer are few and far between. We've had a few good years – 1957, 1976, 1990, 1993, in my memory – but we've also had rotters when it's rained every day in July or when August has been a washout.

Another problem with picnics is that you have to do the work yourself. In France and Italy there sometimes seems so little point. Any small town will have charcuteries, traiteurs, boulangeries and pâtisseries that will provide everything for you, at a cost. You pick up a baguette, some saucisson sec, some oeufs en gêlée, a few tomatoes. Going to a supermarket here is not the same thing: it has none of the pleasure and little of the quality.

The one problem in those countries, though, is huge and well nigh insuperable – insects. I have never had a picnic in France that was not ruined by wasps. We have a thriving wasp population in this country, it's true, but they are like the Swiss navy in comparison to the French strike force.

There's no doubt that a successful picnic depends on an almost unwarranted degree of labour and organisation. However kind the habitat may be, a picnic still involves a mastery of the elements. I have friends who won't have a picnic without building a fire on the beach, such is their boy-scout enthusiasm for the project. At least their chosen beach consists mostly of large, flat rocks, which act as picnic tables and prevent sand getting in the food. Call me a perfectionist or what, but I get little pleasure from chomping through sand in the sandwiches. Woods, glades and fields all have their problems, whether it's ants, wet grass, nettles, thistles or simply the lack of a level surface on which to put a glass of wine.

Undaunted, we blunder on. Here is a picnic of some style that is also manageable. There is no point pretending, however, that there isn't a fair bit of planning involved. If you are intending to have a picnic the day you read this I am afraid you should have started three days ago. Summer pudding is not, in fact, much work, although my recipe is rather long. The peppers take half an hour to put together and the chicken is a doddle.

There's no explaining gastronomic affinities. Sometimes they exist by virtue of association and remembrance rather than for any gustatory reason. We see a leg of lamb and feel impelled to stuff it with garlic and rosemary. Given a loin of pork or a rib of beef, we do not, even though the pork thus treated would be perfectly delicious. Some pairings have become so obvious that we shy away for fear of clichés – duck à l'orange and chicken with tarragon may be good examples. Since both are extremely good combinations, I shall persevere. Picnics and perseverance go together.

PIEDMONTESE PEPPERS

4 red peppers
100g butter
1 clove of garlic
8 basil leaves
8 anchovies
2 tomatoes
Olive oil

The elegance and simplicity of this dish never fail to delight. Its source is the inimitable Elizabeth David, and it exemplifies her sensibility, that perfect pitch that resounds throughout her work.

Cut the peppers down their three or four indentations and around the cores, producing little 'boats'. Remove any seeds or pith. Place them skin-side down and fairly well packed together in a shallow ovenproof dish.

Cut the butter into little cubes and distribute evenly in each boat. Cut the garlic into very fine slivers and add to each one, together with half a basil leaf and half an anchovy.

Peel the tomatoes by plunging them into boiling water for fifteen seconds and then refreshing in cold water. Slice them into rounds or semi-circles, depending on the size of the peppers. Place these slices in the boats on top of the anchovies, garlic, basil and butter. Season with milled pepper and a very little salt.

Bake in an oven preheated to 200°C / Gas Mark 6 for about half an hour, until the peppers have softened but not collapsed. They should be eaten within a couple of hours of coming out of the oven, with plenty of crusty bread.

ROAST CHICKEN WITH TARRAGON

75g unsalted butter, softened
2 teaspoons chopped tarragon, plus a couple of sprigs
2 teaspoons very finely chopped shallot
A 1.5–2kg roasting chicken
2 tablespoons tarragon vinegar
1 glass of white wine
250ml chicken stock

Serve this with cold pilaff rice (see page 79) and a salad of green beans tossed with olive oil, lemon juice and chopped shallot at the last minute.

Mix together the softened butter, chopped tarragon, shallot and half a teaspoon of coarsely milled black pepper. Starting at the neck cavity of the chicken, carefully lift the skin away from the flesh around the breast and force the butter into the gap either side of the breast bone. Pull

the skin back down over the cavity. Put the tarragon sprigs, some milled pepper and plenty of salt into the main cavity of the bird. With clean hands, massage the butter under the breast skin so that it is well distributed and then proceed to truss the bird.

Roast the chicken on one side in an oven preheated to 230°C / Gas Mark 8. After twenty minutes, turn it on its other side and roast for a further twenty minutes. Then turn it on its back, sprinkle with sea salt and reduce the oven temperature slightly. Cook for another twenty minutes or so, by which time the juices from the knee joint should come out clear when pierced with a skewer. Remove the bird from the oven and leave it to rest on a dish that will collect any juices from it.

Pour the juices and butter out of the roasting tin and reserve. Put the tin over the heat and deglaze it with the tarragon vinegar, scraping up any caramelised residue. Boil until the vinegar has almost completely evaporated, then add the white wine. Boil to reduce this by half, then add the stock and transfer to a saucepan.

Separate the fat from the chicken juices as best you can. You can do this by letting them settle a little so the fat rises to the top, then lifting off the fat with a bulb baster, or, if you have a sauceboat with two spouts, one high and one low, you can pour off the juices from the lower spout, leaving the fat behind. Add the juices to the gravy and let this simmer gently until reduced to a nice, clear, gravy consistency. Season with salt and pepper.

Joint the chicken into eight pieces and place them in a picnic container. Collect any juice that has emerged from the chicken and mix with the juices in the pan, then pour this over the chicken.

Leave to cool, then chill for at least two hours. The juices will set to a nice jellied consistency and the chicken will be permeated with the tarragon.

TIAN OF TOMATOES AND AUBERGINES

300g puff pastry
750g aubergines
200ml olive oil, plus extra for dribbling
over the tian
750g ripe tomatoes
1 bunch of parsley
4 cloves of garlic
3 tablespoons breadcrumbs

I am no great shakes at puff pastry so, especially since this is the season for lazy cooking, I have no hesitation in buying it in. Needless to say, this tian is only worth making with good, ripe tomatoes, such as the Italian vine-ripened ones or French Marmande, or plum tomatoes from either country.

Roll out the puff pastry into a disc 26cm in diameter and leave to rest on a baking sheet in the fridge.

Cut the aubergines into slices half a centimetre thick. Toss them in a bowl with the olive oil and then cook in a dry frying pan, brushing them with a little more oil if they become too dry. They should be golden brown and cooked through.

Remove the cores from the tomatoes and peel them by plunging them into boiling water for ten seconds and then refreshing in plenty of cold water. Slip off the skins and slice the tomatoes the same thickness as the aubergines.

Wash the parsley, strip off the leaves and chop them quite finely. Peel the garlic and chop very finely, crushing it with the help of a teaspoon of sea salt. Mix together the garlic, parsley and breadcrumbs to make a persillade.

Arrange the tomatoes and aubergines in overlapping layers on top of the puff pastry, leaving a 1.5cm border of pastry still showing. Season with a little salt and plenty of milled pepper before sprinkling the persillade over the top. Dribble a little oil over the surface and then bake in an oven preheated to 190°C / Gas Mark 5 for thirty-five minutes.

Slide on to a large serving plate and leave to cool.

SUMMER PUDDING

200g redcurrants
700g raspberries
125g caster sugar, plus 1 tablespoon
100g blackcurrants
8 slices of stale white bread, crusts
  removed

People not only argue about which fruit should go in a summer pudding but also whether or not it should be cooked. Most recipes prescribe cooking it, which is, I think, a shame. True, if making it with raw fruit it will take an extra day to macerate the fruit in sugar so that it yields up enough juice, but the fresher, cleaner flavour thus obtained is ample reward. Another cavil concerns the quality of the bread: a good, strong white crumb is required, slightly stale. A sliced loaf is not very clever but anything would be better than brown bread.

Three days may seem a long time to take over a pudding: it is actually the leisurely route, and requires little effort. If you are in more of a hurry, the time for macerating the fruit can be truncated.

Day one

Top and tail the redcurrants and rinse them briefly in cold water. Put them in a bowl with the raspberries and the 125g sugar and mix well. Cover and leave to macerate overnight.

Day two

Put the blackcurrants in a pan with the tablespoon of sugar and two tablespoons of water. Bring gently to the boil, simmer for one minute and then leave to cool. Add them to the raspberries and redcurrants.

Cut a circle out of one of the slices of bread and place in the bottom of a 1.5 litre pudding basin. Cut five slices of bread in half at an angle, creating halves that are almost triangular, with uneven sides. Overlap these slices around the walls of the basin, with the short sides at the base and abutting the piece at the bottom.

Pour all the fruit into the lined mould, reserving a little of the juice. Place a slice of bread on top of the ensemble and bring the tops of the side pieces over to enclose the fruit. A final piece of bread may be needed to make little infills if the top piece is not quite big enough. Place a flat plate that fits inside the rim of the basin over the pudding and place a good heavy weight on top of that. Put the pudding in the fridge for twenty-four hours.

Day three

Remove the weight and plate and invert the pudding on to a serving dish. Holding plate and bowl together, give the combination a couple of quick shakes and the pudding should happily ease itself on to the plate. It should be a glistening, deep crimson colour throughout. Spoon any juice back over the pudding and serve with clotted or double cream.

WHERE DID SUMMER PUDDING COME FROM?

There are no references to this archetypal English dessert by this name prior to 1935 but its history is a long and distinguished one. Although it is sometimes known as a fruit charlotte, I was put on a different track when I read Carol Shields' novel *The Stone Diaries* (1993). The book starts: "My mother's name was Mercy Stone Goodwill. She was only thirty years old when she took sick, a boiling hot day, standing there in her back kitchen, making a Malvern pudding for her husband's supper. A cookery book lay open on the table: 'Take some slices of stale bread,' the recipe said, 'and one pint of currants; half a pint of raspberries; four ounces of sugar; some sweet cream if available...'"

I was intrigued. I could find no references to Malvern pudding in any cookbook in my possession. My English cookery library is an impoverished one, to say the least, but I was still surprised. The story was set in 1905 and the author was emphatic: "The book is an old one, printed in England more than thirty years ago. . ."

Partly as an excuse to correspond with one of my favourite authors, I faxed Carol Shields and asked the identity of the book. After diligently contacting her daughter in Vancouver, to whom she had sent the book, it turned out to be more modern than she had remembered, her edition at least of Warne's *Model Cookery and Housekeeping Book* being published in 1913. Her copy is inscribed, "To Clary from Sister Adelina", who both sound like characters from the novel. Her response was kind but did not take me much closer to the source.

If it wasn't called summer pudding, or even Malvern pudding, what was it called? The answer is quite simple: hydropathic pudding. So easily digestible was the pudding thought to be that it was considered extremely healthy, and may well have started life in a spa town. That spa might have been Malvern; after all, Darwin wrote in his journals: "I went in 1848 for some months to Malvern for hydropathic treatment . . ." The wheel had come full circle. Perhaps it needed the change of name some time between 1930 and 1960 to catch on and become the most popular of English puddings. Somehow, 'hydropathic' pudding doesn't really hit the spot.

ALFRESCO DINNER

GREEK SALAD

ROAST LOIN OF PORK WITH HERBS AND GARLIC

GREENGAGE AND ALMOND TART

Serves 6

I inherited a love of the great outdoors from my father. We're not talking hang-gliding or pony trekking here, ours had rather more to do with table and chairs, bread and wine, reading and conversation. Before the sound of the first cuckoo, my father's voice would boom out, 'Shall we eat outside today?' We generally did. We ate outside any day feasible and Father would munch trenchantly on through drizzle and wind until my mother might call a halt to the proceedings, explaining that she could take a joke but this was ridiculous. Having inherited this alfresco impulse, I make no apologies for staging so many of these menus out of doors.

Even if many people do not have gardens, most of us enjoy eating outside at the slightest opportunity. It is a more relaxed experience than indoor dining: children can run around, babies can throw food from the highchair, smokers can smoke and few need hurry.

It is this sort of relaxed approach that characterises eating in Greece. Only in India have I encountered such a lackadaisical approach to the business of serving food. We do not cook a lot of Greek food in this country, it has about as bad a reputation as any cuisine could have but I have eaten well in Greece. A Greek salad and some grilled sardines is a perfect and very cheap lunch. There are superb mullet and bream on the islands, albeit at a price. A slowly simmered kleftiko or sheftalia can be delicious.

I remember one particular taverna on Cos that used to set up a spit roast in the evenings and do superb chickens, kid and a spectacular loin of pork that I have since copied many times. Dessert, unless you are a devotee of honey, syrup and nuts, is not a Greek strong point, so I have defected to France for the last course. If they have any greengages in Greece, they keep them well hidden.

GREEK SALAD

4 large, ripe tomatoes
1 large cucumber or 2 small ones
250g feta cheese
1 red onion or 6 spring onions
2 tablespoons black olives
1 teaspoon roughly chopped
* marjoram or oregano*
4 tablespoons olive oil

Needless to say, really good, ripe tomatoes are needed here. Look also for the little Italian cucumbers that are firmer and less watery than ours. The Greeks certainly would not peel the tomatoes and I recommend authenticity on this occasion.

Slice the tomatoes and spread them in overlapping rings over a large plate. Peel the cucumber, cut it in slices the thickness of a pound coin and distribute them on top of the tomatoes.

Slice the feta thinly and spread it on top. Cut the onion in thin rounds and place these on top in turn.

Sprinkle with the olives and marjoram or oregano, season with pepper and anoint with the oil. Take to the table and then cut the salad up with a knife and fork before serving.

ROAST LOIN OF PORK WITH HERBS AND GARLIC

1 loin of pork with 5 ribs attached,
* weighing 2–2.5kg*
4 cloves of garlic
1 lemon
1 dessertspoon chopped marjoram
1 dessertspoon chopped mint
½ dessertspoon chopped thyme
1 dessertspoon chopped parsley
2 glasses of white wine

Timing is all with a loin of pork: undercooked, it is repugnant to most sensibilities; overcooked, it becomes dry and flavourless. Timings in a recipe can never be that accurate, and I always use a skewer or meat thermometer to be certain.

Ask the butcher to 'chine' the rack: this should mean cutting through the ribs where they meet the backbone but leaving both attached to the meat. Ask him also to score it very well in parallel lines no more than half a centimetre apart. Peel the garlic cloves and split them in half. With a small, sharp knife, make two small incisions between the ribs about 5cm apart and insert the garlic.

Finely grate the zest of the lemon and mix with the herbs, a teaspoon of sea salt and the same of milled black pepper. Stuff this mixture all along the channel between the ribs and the backbone (you may need to make it deeper for the purpose).

Season with more salt and pepper all the facets of the joint except the skin. This should be rubbed vigorously with the cut face of the lemon, so that it is dripping in juice. Now rub the skin really well with plenty of fine table salt.

Place the pork skin-side up in a baking tray and put it in an oven preheated to 220°C / Gas Mark 7 for twenty minutes. Turn the tray around in the oven so that the crackling gets an even heat and cook for a further twenty minutes.

At this point, pour out all the fat from the tray. Turn the oven down to 190°C / Gas Mark 5 and leave the meat to cook for another twenty minutes. By this time the crackling should be set hard (if not, sprinkle it with a little salt and give the meat ten minutes longer in a hotter oven).

Remove the joint from the oven, take a long, sharp knife and remove all the crackling in one piece. Season the exposed fat on top of the loin, pour the white wine into the baking tray and put back in the oven at 220°C / Gas Mark 7 for twenty minutes. Test the meat with a meat thermometer or a skewer: it should be hot in the centre (75°C). Remove from the tin.

Scrape up the juices in the tin, diluting them with a little water (or stock) – the intention is only to provide a little juice with the meat, not a full-scale gravy. Let the meat rest for ten minutes, then carve it straight down parallel to the ribs, providing alternate slices on and off the bone. Serve with generous pieces of crackling, some potatoes fried in the pork fat and a sharp little Cos lettuce salad.

GREENGAGE AND ALMOND TART

250g fresh greengages
50g blanched almonds
2 tablespoons apricot jelly or sieved
*   apricot jam*

For the pastry:

65g butter
50g caster sugar
1 egg
125g plain flour
For the almond cream:
75g butter
75g caster sugar
2 small eggs
1 dessertspoon dark rum (if available)
50g ground almonds
15g plain flour

An easy tart to make, in as much as the pastry case does not need to be baked blind before filling. It is important to make sure that it is fully cooked, however: I always put the tart on a very hot baking tray to give it a good start.

To make the pastry, cream the butter and sugar together in a food mixer or in a bowl with a wooden spoon. When they are perfectly smooth, mix in the beaten egg to form a wet paste. Sift in the flour with a pinch of salt and fold it in very gently without working the dough. Collect together into a ball, wrap in clingfilm and refrigerate for an hour.

Butter a 26cm loose-bottomed tart tin. Roll out the dough to fit the tin and, collecting it on the rolling pin, drop it into the tin. Push the dough well into the corners and ensure that there is a 1cm overlap all around the edge. Cover with clingfilm and refrigerate for twenty minutes.

For the almond cream, beat the butter and sugar together very well. Mix in the eggs to make a smooth paste, and the rum if desired. Fold in the ground almonds and mix to a smooth dough. Sift in the flour and stir into the mix very gently.

Fill the tart case with a layer of almond cream 1cm thick and no more. Halve the greengages and remove their stones. Place them close together, skin-side down, on the almond cream. Scatter the almonds in the gaps. Bake in an oven preheated to 200°C / Gas Mark 6 for twenty-five minutes. Turn it down to 180°C / Gas Mark 4 and cook for another twenty minutes. Remove the tart from the oven and leave to cool until lukewarm.

Dissolve the jam in a tablespoon of water and paint it over the surface of the tart with a pastry brush to form a shiny glaze. Serve lukewarm, with some cream or crème fraîche.

IT HAD TO GO, I SUPPOSE

Now that a generation of health freaks has learnt to remove the skin from their steamed chicken breasts and the supermarkets are commissioning beef with negligible fat and little marbling, now that sales of low-fat spread match those of butter, what chance has crackling? Despite the extraordinary evidence to the contrary – the famous French paradox, wh ereby the people of south-west France have the highest intake of animal fat and the lowest incidence of heart disease in Europe – the Western world is convinced that animal fat is the root of all evil.

I have a theory that health has got nothing to do with it. It is repugnance. We simply cannot take raw nature in tooth and claw any more. As food becomes increasingly 'product', pre-packaged and divorced from its reality, and as the country becomes a theme park for urbanites rather than a means of sustenance, we are too alienated to cope with the sight of a whole rabbit, a pig's snout or a calf's tongue. I may bang on about it, but who can deny that our larder, our vocabulary of food, is steadily diminishing?

Never mind crackling. In Italy salted pork fat is cut into wafer-thin strips and eaten with salami and prosciutto as an antipasto. Yorkshire bacon used to be similar: great white blocks of fat marbled with thin seams of lean meat were considered a great treat. Whether the incidence of heart disease was higher there than in any other parts of Britain, I very much doubt.

Crackling is not a purely British delicacy. The Chinese are masters at getting pork skin to a quintessence of brittle, wafery crispness that makes our own efforts seem very hit and miss. Unfortunately, the wisdom of millennia is as nothing compared to the pontifications of health faddists, supported and abetted by powerful vested interests.

I N T E R L U D E

RICE

Of the three major staples, I become increasingly fascinated with rice. I know wheat is more versatile, I know many people cannot sit down to a meal without potatoes, but I want to cook rice. It does not matter if it is nutty and creamy arborio or the aromatic and fluffy basmati. They both seem endlessly subtle in their ability to absorb and carry other flavours as well as their own.

RISOTTO MILANESE

A pinch of saffron
1 litre chicken stock
1 onion
80g butter
450g Arborio rice
1 glass of white wine
Lemon juice
100g Parmesan cheese,
  freshly grated
Serves 4–6

This is normally associated with osso bucco but, when made with good stock and fine Parmesan, it is an excellent dish in its own right. Be careful not to overdo the saffron; a small pinch will give a lovely pale gold tinge to the risotto but more will produce a lurid yellow and too overpowering a flavour.

Put the saffron in the chicken stock and bring gently to the boil. Remove from the heat and leave to infuse for fifteen minutes, then bring back to a gentle simmer.

Peel the onion and chop it quite finely. Melt half the butter in a heavy saucepan and sweat the onion in it for five minutes, until soft and translucent. Add the rice, together with a generous pinch of salt. Turn this mixture on a gentle heat until every grain is coated in the butter and the rice starts to stick to the pan.

Add the white wine and stir. As soon as the wine has been absorbed, start to add the hot stock. A ladle at a time, over a gentle heat, stir in the stock and then wait, still stirring, until it has been absorbed before adding more. If you run out of stock before the rice is done, use hot water.

As the risotto proceeds, it can be stirred a little less assiduously but still at regular intervals. This process will take eighteen to twenty minutes.

The rice is cooked when it is, as they say, 'nutty to the bite'. This does not mean that there remains a hard, starchy core but that each grain is separate and is still firm but evenly cooked.

At this point you should act reasonably quickly. As you taste the rice for doneness, check the seasoning. It will probably need a squeeze of lemon juice, plenty of milled black pepper and a pinch of salt. Stir in the remaining butter. The texture now should be very moist but there should be no excess liquid except that held in suspension with the rice and the risotto should not sink across the plate.

Serve immediately, passing around a bowl of the freshly grated Parmesan so that everyone may help themselves.

RISOTTO PRIMAVERA

The same ingredients as the risotto Milanese, omitting the saffron, plus:

200g tiny new spring carrots, about
    1cm in diameter
12 asparagus spears
200g podded broad beans
200g podded peas
Serves 4–6

Although, generally speaking, a good stock is the making of a risotto, this one can be made very well without, just as long as the vegetables are added at the beginning and allowed to flavour the rice, not added at the end as an afterthought.

Wash the carrots well and slice them into 1cm pieces. Trim the asparagus and slice the same size. Drop the broad beans into a pot of boiling water, boil for thirty seconds and then plunge them into a bowl of ice-cold water. Pop the little green beans out of their skins.

Proceed as in the previous recipe. After the onion has been sweated down add the carrots, asparagus and peas (unless the latter are exceptionally tender, in which case they should be added later, with the broad beans) and turn them in the butter. Add the rice and proceed as before, adding the broad beans five minutes before the end.

COURGETTE AND GORGONZOLA RISOTTO

The same ingredients as the risotto Milanese, omitting the saffron and reducing the butter to 40g, plus:

350g courgettes
100g Gorgonzola cheese
Serves 4–6

I feel sorry for those who think courgettes lack taste. There is no pretence of keeping them *al dente* here: they will be quite mushy and will have rendered all their flavour to the rice.

Cut the courgettes into halfcentimetre cubes. Proceed as for the risotto Milanese, adding the courgettes at the same time as the rice.

Stew a little longer together and use a little less stock, as the courgettes contain plenty of water of their own.

Grate or chop the Gorgonzola and stir it into the risotto as it finishes. Omit the final butter enrichment but still offer plenty of Parmesan.

POTATO, FENNEL AND ROSEMARY RISOTTO

The same ingredients as the risotto Milanese, omitting the saffron, plus:

100g pancetta
1 fennel bulb
250g peeled potatoes
A sprig of rosemary
Serves 4–6

It may seem odd to have starches together, but potatoes are as wonderful in a risotto as they are with pasta or pulses.

Cut the pancetta into small dice, no bigger than half a centimetre. Trim the fennel and

cut it to the same size, saving the green tops. Cut the potatoes slightly larger.

Proceed as for risotto Milanese but cook the pancetta in the butter first, until it takes a little colour and is sealed on every side, then add the fennel and the onion together.

Add the potatoes with the rice and the rosemary at the same time as the wine. If the rosemary flavour begins to get too powerful, remove it.

Finish in the usual way, when the rice is cooked and the potatoes have begun to break up.

PILAFF

Enough basmati rice to fill a measuring jug up to 400ml

1 onion
1 clove of garlic
100g unsalted butter
2 sprigs of thyme
Serves 4–6

By all means substitute chicken stock for water if you want to make a richer, more flavoured pilaff, but I love it plain, like this, in all its serene simplicity.

Place the rice in a bowl and pour over a full kettle of boiling water. Stir momentarily with a fork and leave to stand for ten minutes, then drain well and rinse in cold water. Alternatively, simply rinse the rice in several changes of cold water and drain well.

Peel the onion and chop it very finely. Peel the clove of garlic. Melt half the butter in a heavy pan that has a tight-fitting lid. Add the onion and the whole garlic clove and let them sweat gently until the onion becomes translucent. Add the welldrained rice to the pot, turning it several times so that each grain is coated in butter. Add the thyme, two very good pinches of salt and 600ml of cold water. Bring quickly to the boil, stirring only a little, and then reduce the heat to very low, cover and leave to cook for eleven minutes.

Remove the pilaff from the heat. Add the rest of the butter and gently fork it through the rice. Replace the lid and leave the rice to stand for ten minutes.

PRAWN BIRYANI

500g frozen tiger prawns in their shells, defrosted
1 dessertspoon coriander seeds
1 dessertspoon fennel seeds
6 cardamom pods
12 peppercorns
2 onions
50g fresh root ginger
4 cloves of garlic
1 tablespoon sunflower oil
50g butter, plus a knob
1 cinnamon stick
1.5 litres water
500g basmati rice
½ teaspoon chilli flakes
Grated zest and juice of 1 lime
2 tablespoons chopped coriander leaves

Serves 4–6

However much I love a good risotto, nothing approaches basmati rice for delicacy of flavour and texture. It needs careful washing, the right ratio of liquid (3:2 is my golden rule) and must not be overcooked.

Peel the prawns, reserving the shells. Keep the bodies in a covered bowl in the fridge.

Crush the coriander, fennel, cardamom and peppercorns roughly in a mortar, spice mill or blender. Peel and thinly slice one of the onions, together with the ginger and garlic.

Heat the oil in a heavy saucepan and add the prawn shells. Colour the shells briskly for a few minutes until they start to dry up and stick to the pan. Add half the butter and the ground spices and turn these until they form a sticky paste.

Add the sliced onion, ginger and garlic, the cinnamon stick and water. Bring to the boil and simmer this stock for one hour, then strain and set aside.

Measure the volume of the rice in a measuring jug before transferring it to a fine sieve. Wash the rice copiously in several changes of cold water until the water is no longer cloudy. Drain very well.

Peel the second onion and chop it finely. Melt the remaining butter in a casserole, add the onion and let it soften gently before adding the rice.

Turn the rice in the butter before adding exactly one and a half times its measured volume in stock. Add a generous pinch of sea salt and bring to the boil. Stir well, cover and place in an oven preheated to 200°C / Gas Mark 6 for twelve minutes.

When the rice is almost cooked, slice the prawns in half lengthways and mix with the chilli flakes, the grated lime zest and juice and the fresh coriander. Remove the rice from the oven and stir in the prawns and their little marinade. Add the knob of butter and replace the lid of the casserole.

Simply leave the biryani to stand for six or seven minutes so that the prawns cook in the heat of the rice. Serve with a crisp green salad.

AUTUMN

THE CLUB DINNER FOR THE RICH UNCLE

MUSHROOM GATHERERS' LUNCH

SUPPER PARTY

HALLOWE'EN NIGHT: TRICKS AND TREATS

A VEGETARIAN LUNCH

AUTUMN

Summer food is all very well. I love the 'Mediterranean diet', I love salads and simple food but in September food gets serious again. It's not just the cook that gets lazy in summer. The appetite switches off a little, too. In autumn our gastronomic curiosity revives. The stimuli are there, after all. It is undoubtedly my favourite time to cook. I feel sorry at any time, but especially in September, for those who pooh-pooh the notion of seasonality and strive for a consistent year-round cuisine. How sad not to be excited by the beginning of the game season, the return of shellfish – especially oysters – to the menu, and the arrival of autumn fruit and wild mushrooms such as ceps and girolles.

I cannot believe there is another country in the world with the quality of game we have in this country. Grouse, wild duck,

partridge, pheasant and woodcock follow each other in successive waves as each achieves maturity and is shot, hung and prepared for the table.

Personally, I could never shoot a grouse. I am such an appalling marksman that were I to patrol the finest moors for weeks on end I would be unlikely to bag a single bird. I am also temperamentally unsuited to killing game. This is not some kind of moral stance: I simply want someone else to do the killing for me. My father was a decent shot but had the same problem. We had a small piece of land in Northern Ireland that was plagued by magpies. My father decided to deal with the pests. The first day he he bagged a moorhen by mistake. I can still see him now, looking dolefully down at the fine blue and black livery of the innocent waterbird. We never saw his gun in action again.

For all my squeamishness, I will defend endlessly those who do shoot. There's little question that, without the protection and encouragement of gamekeepers and the whole shooting fraternity, there would be few of these birds left. The foothold a grouse, for example, has on life is precarious anyway: without the sport they would surely cease to exist altogether. We are more careful and protective of our game birds in this country than others. The French, Spanish and, worst of all, Italians are so indiscriminate and so wholesale in their slaughter that there are few birds left to shoot.

In a similar burst of chauvinistic pride, there is not an oyster to compare with the native round oyster. Its rich, full, meaty flavour is, to my mind, of a higher order than all others. Its existence has also been under threat. That depth of flavour is only achieved at the expense of much longer breeding periods (three to five years for a native, one to two for a rock) and, in years past, oyster farmers were reluctant to make such an investment. Pollution has also taken its toll of the traditional breeding grounds. The situation has much improved in recent years, however: the Irish have taken the lead but there are signs that others in this country have followed suit.

In other areas things are looking up, too. Old varieties of apples and pears have been revived and it is becoming understood that growing fruit 'for flavour' has some merit. Wild mushrooms have begun to be harvested on a commercial scale, although it will always be more exciting and a great deal less expensive if one picks them oneself. All in all, it is not a bad time to be a cook.

THE CLUB DINNER
FOR THE RICH UNCLE

OYSTER AND ONION TART

ROAST GROUSE WITH BREAD SAUCE

MIRABELLES AND CUSTARD
Serves 4

There's something rather incongruous about the grouse season. I suppose it has always started so early in order to give the Hoorays something to do in August. The poor creatures can't go to the beach like the rest of us – that would be much too common – so they go north to the great estates to do a bit of shootin' and fishin'. Most of the salmon have finished their run, so the grouse get it in the neck. These days, of course, a day's shooting fetches such a price that your grouse is more likely to be shot by some psychopath in borrowed tweeds from Dallas or Düsseldorf than by any homebred assassin. I don't care who shoots them as long as I don't have to do

it and as long as somebody does, for no finer meat can be placed on the table.

Far from trying to get the birds on the Glorious Twelfth (a ridiculous ritual performed by a few London hotels, since even the tenderest young birds should be hung for at least a couple of days), I would rather wait a couple of weeks and start eating grouse at the beginning of September. The birds will be a little plumper and we will be more in the mood. Grouse has a rich, gamy flavour and, to my mind, its dark meat is more suited to the autumn menu than the summer one.

September, of course, also means the beginning of the oyster season. When asked what is my favourite meal, I invariably reply with this archetypal menu of oysters and grouse. Ideally, the oysters would be half a dozen (all right, make it a dozen) natives, raw and with nothing more than a squeeze of lemon and a twist of black pepper. Since natives have become so prohibitively expensive and this is supposed to be a cookbook

I offer this excellent oyster and onion tart in their place.

As for the mirabelles, they are hardly traditional clubland fare. They are, admittedly, not easily come by. The best are from France around the middle of August and, when they are blushing red and bursting with sweetness, there is nothing to touch them. They are the finest plums imaginable and only the little greengages that arrive around the same time begin to approach them for flavour: by all means use them if mirabelles are not available.

I include mirabelles here for three reasons: it is their season, they can be bottled very successfully, and an old-fashioned plate of stewed fruit with custard will have the uncle waxing lyrical about his schooldays and put him in an even more amenable mood.

This is an expensive menu. If you offer it to a rich uncle, he'll be very gratified and there could be a return on the investment. There's no point in offering it to those who are nervous or squeamish about their food: such a sacrifice would be pearls before swine.

OYSTER AND ONION TART

24 oysters
1 pint of periwinkles (a teacupful when picked)
3 large white onions 1
00ml double cream
75g unsalted butter
Lemon juice
1 tablespoon very finely chopped chives

For the pastry:

200g plain flour
100g unsalted butter

Although they are hardly essential to the dish, the periwinkles are a nice touch. Getting them out of their shell is child's play compared to oysters. All you need is a pin and a child to bribe to do the work. If you are not adept with oysters, and have no wish to be so, ask your fishmonger to unhinge them without actually removing the shells – they must be used the same day if opened in this way, however.

For the pastry, mix the flour with a pinch of salt in a bowl. Cut the butter into very small cubes, keeping it cold. Rub these into the flour and work with your fingertips until the mixture has a breadcrumb texture. Make a well in the middle and add two tablespoons of cold water. Gently knead the mixture with your fingertips to form a dough. If it will not hold together, add a little more water but be cautious. Gather into a ball, cover with clingfilm and refrigerate for half an hour.

Roll out the pastry into a disc slightly larger than your tart tin, which should be 26 – 28cm in diameter. Collect the pastry on the rolling pin and unroll it into the tin. Make sure that the pastry goes right into the sides and also overhangs the lip of the tin.

Do not trim off this overhang at this juncture. Line the tart with some greaseproof paper or aluminium foil and fill with dried beans. Bake in an oven preheated to 190°C / Gas Mark 5 for twenty minutes, then remove the beans and paper and cook the pastry for another five minutes. The base should be completely cooked. Remove from oven and cut off pastry overhang. Keep the oven on.

Open the oysters and lift out the meat on to a plate. Collect all the juice in a bowl and dip each oyster in it to rinse off any bits of shell. Strain the juice through a fine sieve into a small saucepan. Pick the periwinkles out of their shells.

Peel the onions, quarter them, and drop them into plenty of boiling salted water.

Let them simmer briskly for ten minutes or until they are completely tender. Drain the onions and return them to the pan, stirring briefly over a medium heat to remove any excess water.

Add half the cream, bring briskly to the boil, then remove from the heat as soon as the cream starts to thicken. Put this mixture into a blender and whizz to a very smooth purée. Season the purée with milled white pepper and spoon it into the tart case. It should form a layer half a centimetre deep. Put the tart back in the warm oven with the door ajar.

Bring the oyster juice up to a simmer and drop in the oysters. The oysters should poach for barely half a minute per side. The minute they start to plump up and stiffen, lift them out and, once well drained, distribute on top of the onion purée. Continue to keep warm.

Add the periwinkles to the oyster liquor and warm them briefly before draining them in turn and sprinkling amongst the oysters.

ROAST GROUSE

150g streaky bacon or pork fat
4 grouse
50g butter
1 level teaspoon plain flour
1 glass of white wine
300ml chicken stock
A sprig of thyme (or summer savory)

If the butcher has not already done so, wrap the bacon or pork fat over the breasts of the grouse, secure in place with string and truss the birds. Melt the butter in a heavy ovenproof pan on top of the stove and brown the birds on all sides for a couple of minutes. Place them on their backs and transfer to an oven preheated to 240°C / Gas Mark 9. Roast for twelve to fifteen minutes. Feel each bird between thumb and forefinger at the base of the breasts, just above the wingtips: it should be quite firm and resilient to the touch – if still soft, they will be too rare. Turn the grouse on to their breasts and let them rest on a warm plate while you make a little gravy.

Pour the fat out of the pan and sprinkle in the flour. Let this brown, stirring and scraping up the pan residue with a wooden spoon. Pour in the white wine. Continue to scrape up all the juices from the pan while the wine simmers and reduces by half, then add the chicken stock, thyme and some salt and pepper. Let this in turn reduce by half.

Remove the string from the grouse. Pour any juices from the plate or from inside the grouse into the gravy. If you are using pork fat, remove and discard it, but leave bacon on the birds. Strain the gravy into a sauceboat. Serve the grouse with the gravy, bread sauce, some breadcrumbs fried in butter (purely optional in my opinion) and some game chips (I have no compunction in serving good potato crisps, as long as they are unflavoured). Some runner beans or early Brussels sprouts will not go amiss.

BREAD SAUCE

½ large white loaf
1 onion
8 cloves
500ml milk
2 bay leaves
2 large sprigs of thyme
A pinch of grated nutmeg
100ml double cream

I adore bread sauce, hot or cold. A cold partridge with some leftover bread sauce and a little redcurrant jelly is the perfect Sunday supper. The bread should be at least a day old.

Remove the crusts from the bread and cut or tear the crumb into small pieces; let them dry out a little if too soft and fresh. Peel the onion, stud it with the cloves and put it in a small saucepan with the milk, bay leaves, thyme, nutmeg and some salt and pepper.

Bring to the boil and then remove from the heat and let it stand for twenty minutes to infuse. Add the bread, bring very gently back to the boil and simmer on the very gentlest heat for twenty minutes, stirring occasionally to make sure the sauce does not catch. Lift out the thyme, bay leaves and onion.

Pour in the cream and bring briefly back to the boil, whisking very well. Check the seasoning. Without being lumpy, the sauce should have a nice coarse texture to it and not be too suave or creamy.

MIRABELLES AND CUSTARD

1 vanilla pod
150g caster sugar
500ml white wine
1kg fresh mirabelles
For the custard:
1 vanilla pod
500ml milk
4 large egg yolks
75g caster sugar

Split the vanilla pod in half, put it in a pan with the sugar and white wine and bring to the boil. Add the mirabelles and simmer for two minutes. Remove from the stove and leave to cool.

For the custard, split the vanilla pod and add it to the milk in a small saucepan. Bring to simmering point, then remove from the heat and leave to infuse for fifteen minutes.

Beat together the egg yolks and sugar in a bowl. Reheat the milk to boiling point and add a little less than half of it to the egg yolks and sugar in a thin stream, whisking well. Return this mixture to the rest of the milk in the pan and cook very gently, stirring with a wooden spoon and taking care to get into the corners and across the base of the pan.

Within a minute or two the custard will imperceptibly thicken just enough to coat the back of the spoon. Remove from the heat immediately, continue to stir for a moment and then strain into a bowl and chill.

Serve the mirabelles with a little of their syrup and pour over a little of the custard from a jug.

BOTTLING MIRABELLES

If you are lucky enough to find really good mirabelles, it is well worth bottling a few, which requires no extra effort and is delicious for quick suppers in the weeks ahead.

Poach the fruit as in the preceding recipe and leave to cool. Sterilise some Kilner or Le Parfait jars by removing the rubber seals and passing both jars and seals through the hot cycle of a dishwasher. Replace the seals and lay out the jars on kitchen paper.

Fill the jars, leaving 2cm from the top, and wipe the rims with a very clean cloth dipped in hot water. Fasten the clips if using a Le Parfait style of jar, or screw down the Kilner type.

Place a thick layer of newspaper on the bottom of the largest pan available and carefully place the jars on this. Cover the jars with cold water and bring to the boil. Simmer gently for half an hour and then let cool in the water.

There should be a strong vacuum inside the jars that will prevent any spoilage through oxidation. Store in a cool, dark place.

'I WANTED THE GROUSE'

One of the things that most annoys me, both as a chef and a fellow diner, is the notion that everyone must eat something different. It's a kind of window-shopping mentality, a bit like those ridiculous menus dégustation of eight or ten tiny courses that offer a little bit of everything and not very much of anything.

As a chef, this straining for difference makes life a great deal more difficult. A table of six, with six different starters and six different main courses, is a nightmare. One of the reasons French restaurants used to be so much better than English ones is that the French are not so food obsessed. This may sound heresy but in France a table of six will usually spend a few moments glancing at and discussing the menu, then all order the same thing and start talking about something else. They won't look at the *à la carte* because they know very well it represents poor value and they trust the chef, whose energies, they know, will have gone into the *menu du jour*. The result is that the kitchen does a better job with less staff and using the best and most seasonal ingredients and everyone is happy. The table of convives share the same pleasure, no one feels hard done by and the chef is on the beach by two thirty.

MUSHROOM GATHERERS' LUNCH

PARMA HAM WITH FIGS

WILD MUSHROOM RISOTTO

POTATO AND CEP CAKE

POACHED PEARS IN BEAUJOLAIS WITH CINNAMON ICE CREAM

Serves 6

I remember watching an episode in the telly series featuring the adorable and much missed Jennifer Paterson and Clarissa Dickson Wright, uncharitably called 'Two Fat Ladies'. They were out in the woods picking mushrooms. It was like Dingly Dell. Every type of mushroom – cep, shaggy ink cap, hedgehog, chanterelle and naughty old fly agaric – was poking up and screaming for attention, begging to be picked. It was more like the pick 'n' mix at Woolworth's than any experience I have had picking mushrooms.

There are the great mycophiles like Antonio Carluccio, Pierre Koffmann and Mauro Bregoli, who cannot walk into a wood without kilo upon kilo of perfect ceps practically falling into their laps. And there is me. I have had some success, do not get me wrong. In the Chilterns I picked nearly a kilo of *trompettes de la mort* (I prefer the French name to the English horn of plenty; it's more resonant and the latter is inaccurate – Horn of Not Very Much at All Actually would be nearer the mark) and have enjoyed other minor successes. If I had to rely on my mushroom picking for nourishment, however, I would cut a much slimmer figure than I do today.

Like chasing the fox, the hunt's the thing. Mushroom picking is as full of lore and secrecy as any Masonic lodge. Good friends suddenly turn cold and evasive at the slightest enquiry as to the location of their trove. Directions as precise as "in the south of England" or "an hour away from my parents' place" begin to sound like real clues. These same people get up ridiculously early to beat each other to their quarry. This may be my problem: I've always found it hard to get much accomplished before about eleven o'clock, by which time most pickers have got back home, identified their crop, had breakfast and finished The Times crossword.

Still, it makes a good day out, and the kids love it. Do I need to offer the usual strictures? Of course you must not eat anything until you are absolutely sure you know what it is, and never put anything in a common basket until you are equally sure of its identity. Common sense, really.

Given my difficulties with mushrooms, I've opted for a nice generic dish, the risotto, for our lunch. If you happen to collect a particularly good crop of ceps, make the potato and cep cake. If you are not so lucky in your hunt, fake it with dried ceps, like a disappointed angler's surreptitious visit to a fishmonger.

PARMA HAM WITH FIGS

400g Parma ham
9–12 ripe figs, depending on size, cut into quarters

I never know whether I prefer my Parma ham with figs or with melon – I adore both. This is the time when one has to bully at the delicatessen counter. Make sure the ham is cut from the middle and that it is cut wafer thin. The figs must be soft and ripe and good crusty bread and unsalted butter at hand.

Simply lay out the ham on a big platter, surround it with quartered figs and serve.

WILD MUSHROOM RISOTTO

750g miscellaneous wild mushrooms
1 onion
2 cloves of garlic
1 litre chicken stock
100g butter
450g arborio rice
150g Parmesan, freshly grated

Prepare the mushrooms by trimming the bases, scraping the stalks and cutting off any bits that are rotting. Wash the mushrooms in cold water but do not let them soak. Slice them so that they are all roughly the same size. Peel the onion and garlic and chop quite finely.

Put the stock in a pot and bring gently to the boil. Put half the butter in a heavy saucepan, add the onion and garlic and stew on a gentle heat for five minutes, then add the rice. Stir to coat it well in the butter, then add the mushrooms.

Start slowly adding the stock, stirring as you do so. Add a little more stock every three minutes or so, after each batch has been absorbed by the rice. The mushrooms will start to render their juice, which will help to moisten and flavour the risotto. Continue until the rice is cooked but still slightly nutty to the bite. If you run out of stock before the rice is done, use hot water. Season well and add the rest of the butter. When the whole is completely amalgamated, serve with the Parmesan.

POTATO AND CEP CAKE

125g dried ceps
150g unsalted butter
2 cloves of garlic
25ml olive oil
750g large potatoes
75g Gruyère cheese, grated

If using fresh ceps you will need at least 250g. Slice them, season well and stew gently in a little olive oil for ten minutes. They will absorb any liquid and can be put straight into the cake once cooled.

Soak the ceps in cold water for four hours, then drain. Take a straightsided, round ovenproof dish 20cm in diameter and at least 6cm deep and grease with half the butter, taking special care that the base is well covered.

Peel the garlic and chop it very finely. Warm the olive oil in a frying pan, gently stew the garlic in it for a minute and then add the drained ceps. Let these stew and soften over a low heat, turning them occasionally, for about twenty minutes, until tender. Season and leave to cool.

Peel the potatoes and cut them into rounds the thickness of a two pence piece. Do not wash these slices as the starch on them will help keep them together. Overlap slices of potato in the base of the dish to make a nice pattern. Season the potatoes, dot with some of the remaining butter and distribute a few ceps on top, then sprinkle with a little cheese. Continue to layer the potatoes, buttering and seasoning them a little each time, with the mushrooms and cheese, finishing with a layer of potatoes. Cover with a butter paper or some buttered foil and put on the bottom shelf of an oven preheated to 240°C / Gas Mark 9 for forty-five minutes. Test the potatoes with a knife and then run the knife around he inside of the dish. Let the cake settle or five minutes before inverting it on to a plate. The potatoes should be a crisp, golden brown on the outside and creamy within. Serve with a green salad with some frizzy endive and a sharp dressing.

POACHED PEARS IN BEAUJOLAIS

6 large pears, approaching ripeness
Juice of 1 lemon
1 bottle of Beaujolais
200g caster sugar, or more to taste
1 cinnamon stick
4 cloves
12 black peppercorns
3 strips of lemon zest
3 strips of orange zest
2 tablespoons redcurrant jelly

Carefully peel the pears, leaving the stalks on, and roll them in the lemon juice. Combine the wine, sugar, spices and strips of zest in a saucepan and bring to the boil. Simmer gently for fifteen minutes. Add the pears and poach very gently for fifteen minutes, or longer if they are less ripe. Lift the pears out of the liquor into a serving bowl. Strain the liquor, put it back in the pan and boil until reduced by a third. Whisk in the redcurrant jelly and pour it over the pears. Leave to cool.

Serve cold with cream, vanilla ice cream or the delicious cinnamon version next.

CINNAMON ICE CREAM

2 cinnamon sticks
750ml milk
10 egg yolks
200g caster sugar
250ml double cream

No substitute for the ice-cream machine here, I'm afraid.

Break the cinnamon sticks in half and place them in a saucepan with the milk. Bring to the boil, then remove from the heat and leave to infuse for twenty minutes.

Beat the egg yolks and sugar together very thoroughly. Bring the infused milk back to the boil and pour about a third of it in a slow trickle over the egg yolks and sugar, whisking constantly. Pour this mixture back into the pan, whisking well.

Place on a gentle heat and stir with a wooden spoon until it starts to thicken. Remove it from the heat immediately, strain into a bowl and leave to cool.

Whip the cream until it thickens and leaves a trail off the end of the whisk. Pour in the cold cinnamon custard and whisk until it is completely mixed.

Churn in an ice-cream machine until thick, then freeze.

I'D SOONER DRINK WINE THAN COOK IT MOST OF THE TIME

Whereas there's no point cooking with really awful wine, I see even less point in cooking with anything really good.

Winemakers spend a great deal of effort to arrive at a harmonious balance of sweetness and acidity, of fruit and tannin, which is dissipated practically the minute you put the wine in the pot. Some of the quality of the wine will manifest itself but it seems a terrible shame to fork out the money for something and not appreciate its merits first hand. I could as easily pour Côte Rotie into the oxtail as give caviar to the cat.

The reason the Beaujolais cook pears in their wine is because they have so much of it. The wine was said to be one of the three rivers flowing through Lyons. It even used to be cheap and cheerful here, too, in the days before it was marketed under more serious villages names such as Fleurie and Chiroubles and before they started flogging the new vintage as Beaujolais Nouveau.

If you are going to cook a wine with cinnamon, lemon zest, pepper and sugar, it would be better to choose something more honest and half the price, and it wouldn't really matter if it was Bulgarian Merlot, South African Pinotage or Argentinian Malbec, as long as the thing had a bit of fruit and was not going to break the bank.

SUPPER PARTY

ESCAROLE, PEAR AND ROQUEFORT SALAD

VENISON STEW WITH BABY ONIONS, CHESTNUTS AND CHOCOLATE

POLENTA

GRILLED PINEAPPLE WITH CHILLI SYRUP AND COCONUT ICE CREAM

Serves 12

Do you know who's coming to dinner? Most of the time you probably do – after all, you have invited them. There are occasions, though, when you cannot be so sure, occasions when people 'come on' after a drinks party, a carol concert, the school play or a meeting of the entertainments committee.

If it could be six, eight or twelve, you have to be flexible, not just with the portioning but with the timing as well. One of the many beauties of a stew is that it may take a long time to cook but it is endlessly patient as to when it is served. For some reason, however, stews are not often good in restaurants. It is a numbers thing: a stew keeps beautifully en masse but does not break down into individual portions nearly so well. That said, it takes a degree of confidence to serve a stew. Done badly, the meat tough and insufficiently cooked, or falling apart from overcooking, the sauce pitiably thin or a thick sludge, they are not without their pitfalls. Those strictures aside, once mastered, stews are the easiest of dishes to serve.

A good salad is an excellent way to start a meal. One has to admire the American sense of dietary sufficiency which means that many of them can conceive no other start to a meal than a green salad. Monotonous, maybe, but consistent. Personally, I prefer a green salad at the end of a meal, somewhere between mopping up the juice from a steak and starting on a runny piece of Brie. I like my 'appetiser' salad to be a bit more interesting. That does not mean 'creative' salads, that lop together any number of ingredients in the hope that they will work, but rather careful conjunctions of two or three ingredients that really complement each other. I love combinations of green leaves and cheese, such as Caesar salad or a mustardy curly endive salad with hard-boiled eggs and Gruyère, or the lovely autumnal salad below of milky but slightly bitter escarole leaves with pears and Roquefort cheese.

A large salad is certainly a very useful thing for a home cook, since it can mostly be put together an hour or so ahead, just as long as the dressing is done at the last minute.

Things hot up on this menu with a little chilli to alleviate the richness of the venison and its sauce, and then more chilli in its sensational pairing with pineapple. I make no apologies for this assault: both combinations are subtle, and there is no harm in spicing up a party by stealth.

ESCAROLE, PEAR AND ROQUEFORT SALAD

4 escarole
4 lemons
6 Comice pears
400g Roquefort cheese
4 teaspoons Dijon mustard
2 dessertspoons white wine vinegar
4 tablespoons virgin olive oil

Some might be tempted to add walnuts to such a seasonal combination but I think it better, on balance, without.

Turn the escarole over so its stalk is towards you and its leaves splayed out on the chopping board. With a small, sharp knife cut away the frill of coarse green leaves and then cut away the outside stems as they come towards the stalk. Cut away the stalk and proceed to separate the leaves, cutting them into large pieces. Wash the leaves in a copious amount of cold water and dry in a salad spinner or with colanders and dry cloths.

Squeeze the juice from the lemons into a bowl. Peel the pears and roll them in the juice. Cut them in half, remove the cores and stalks, cut them into long, thin slices and return them to the lemon juice.

Put the cheese on a plate, cover with clingfilm and place in the freezer for ten minutes. Make a dressing by mixing the mustard with half a teaspoon of sea salt and half a teaspoon of milled black pepper, dissolving them in the white wine vinegar and then whisking in the olive oil.

Put the escarole in a salad bowl with the pears. Slice the cheese as thinly as possible and add to the bowl.

Pour over the dressing and then gently turn and fold the mixture until it is completely dressed.

VENISON STEW WITH BABY ONIONS, CHESTNUTS AND CHOCOLATE

3kg stewing venison, cut from the
   shoulder, neck or haunch
1 cup olive oil
2 dessertspoons plain flour
500g button onions
150g unsalted butter
1 dessertspoon sugar
250g peeled chestnuts
15–25g extra-bitter chocolate
1 lemon

For the marinade:

3 large carrots
3 onions
3 sticks of celery
6 cloves of garlic
1 red chilli

6 juniper berries
20 black peppercorns
4 cloves
2 bay leaves
A large sprig of thyme
2 large strips of lemon zest
1 large strip of orange zest
1 cup of red wine vinegar
2 bottles of red wine
¼ cup olive oil

Cooking with chocolate is a dangerous business: a pinch too much and the whole edifice topples over, the chocolate flavour becoming suddenly much too dominant and the sauce cloying and sickly. Used correctly, however, the chocolate gives a marvellously subtle taste – dry, smoky and slightly bitter – and will not be instantly identifiable. Use the bestquality extra-bitter, high-cocoa-fat chocolate that you can lay your hands on and add it cautiously. If you do go over the top, reach for the lemon, the salt and the pepper mill and all will not be lost.

This is quite a laborious dish but can be prepared a day ahead, up to the point before the chocolate is added, and will actually improve for being reheated.

Trim the meat and cut it into large, walnut-sized cubes if the butcher has not already done so.

For the marinade, peel the carrots and onions and cut them, with the celery, into 1cm cubes. Separate the garlic cloves (do not peel), seed and coarsely slice the chilli and put all the ingredients into a large bowl with the meat, finishing with a film of the oil. Cover and leave to marinate overnight in the fridge.

The next day, pour the marinade into a colander placed over a bowl. Lift out the meat and dry it on kitchen paper. Season with sea salt and then brown it in the olive oil in a frying pan, in batches, transferring it to a large ovenproof casserole as each batch is done.

When all the meat has been well browned, fry the vegetables from the marinade in the same pan, turning them frequently. When the vegetables are nicely coloured, sprinkle over the flour and cook for a minute or two until it is also lightly browned.

Pour over the liquid from the marinade and scrape up the residue on the base of the pan with a wooden spoon. As soon as the marinade comes to the boil, pour it over the meat in the casserole. Add a little water if the meat is not well covered, put it on the stove and bring back to the boil, skimming very well to remove any scum or grease that comes to the surface.

Place the casserole in an oven preheated to 170°C / Gas Mark 3 for two hours, until the meat is intact but quite tender. Leave to cool for twenty minutes.

Soak the button onions in warm water for twenty minutes and then peel them, trimming the stems neatly at the base so that they remain intact. Melt 50g of the butter in a frying pan or sauté pan and add the onions. Let them colour gently on all sides before adding the sugar. Let this caramelise a little, then pour in just enough water to cover the onions. Cover with a butter paper and cook for fifteen minutes or until the onions are tender and the liquid has evaporated.

Put the peeled chestnuts in a saucepan with 50g of the butter and enough cold water to cover. Stew very gently, covered, for thirty minutes or until soft.

Drain the stew in a colander over a bowl. Lift out all the pieces of meat and put them back in the casserole. Strain the liquid through a fine sieve back over the meat, squeezing through every drop of juice but discarding the vegetables. Add the onions and chestnuts to the stew (it can be prepared ahead up to this point).

Bring the stew very gently back to a simmer, and cook equally gently for five minutes so the flavours meld and come together. Finely grate the chocolate and whisk in a teaspoon at a time so that it melts into the stew. Proceed cautiously, tasting each time, adding a little chocolate, a knob of the remaining butter, a little squeeze of lemon juice and a pinch of salt. Do not let the chocolate boil. It should give an indefinable subtlety and richness to the stew: the minute you think you can taste the chocolate, stop immediately and correct with a little more lemon juice. When you are content with the balance and the seasoning, serve forthwith, with crispy polenta.

POLENTA

1.5 litres water
250g polenta flour
Olive oil

Polenta is not the most popular of foods. I blame the instant stuff, which bears even less resemblance to real polenta than Smash does to mashed potatoes. Proper polenta flour has the texture of coarse sand, takes almost three-quarters of an hour to cook and ends up with a lovely, rich texture and flavour. Wrongheaded friends claim, "It's what you put in it" – butter, cheese or cream – "that makes it so." This is poppycock.

Old hands won't bother with the measuring jug. If the bubbling lava gets too thick to stir, it can be diluted with more water at any time.

Put the water in a pan, salt well and bring to the boil. Armed with a strong metal whisk, slowly pour in the polenta, stirring constantly as you do so. When all the polenta has been added, continue to stir until the mixture starts to bubble and erupt. Switch to a heavy wooden spoon, scraping the sides of the pan, and turn the heat down very low. Leave to cook very gently, stirring occasionally.

After about forty minutes the polenta will be very thick and start to come away in a mass from the sides of the pan. Season the polenta well with sea salt and plenty of coarsely milled black pepper.

Line a shallow baking tray with buttered greaseproof paper and pour in the polenta to a depth of 1.5 cm. Smooth the surface flat with a palette knife, brush it with a little olive oil and let it cool completely.

Lift it out of the tray, peel off the greaseproof paper and cut the polenta into squares or wedges. Brush the pieces with olive oil and place under a hot grill until bubbling, golden brown and crisp.

GRILLED PINEAPPLE WITH CHILLI SYRUP AND COCONUT ICE CREAM

4 red chillies, medium strength
1 vanilla pod
200g caster sugar
6 star anise
1 bay leaf
300ml water
50ml dark rum
2 pineapples

For the ice cream:

750ml milk
200g finely grated fresh coconut or
*   100g desiccated coconut*
100g creamed coconut
8 egg yolks
150g caster sugar
250ml double cream

First make the ice cream: put the milk and both types of coconut in a saucepan, bring to the boil, then remove from the heat and leave to steep for twenty minutes. Blend in a liquidiser and then return to the heat. Whisk together the egg yolks and sugar in a bowl. When the milk and coconut mixture returns to the boil, pour it into the egg yolk mixture, whisking constantly, and then return the combination to the saucepan. Without letting the mixture get near boiling point, stir constantly until it starts to thicken very slightly. Remove from the heat immediately and continue to stir very thoroughly in the pan for one minute before straining it through a fine sieve into a bowl. Allow to cool, then chill.

Whip the double cream until it thickens and leaves a ribbon effect off the end of the whisk. Fold the coconut mixture into the cream and, when thoroughly mixed, freeze in an ice-cream machine.

For the chilli syrup, split the chillies and remove the seeds under the cold tap. Cut the chillies into very fine, short strips. Split the vanilla pod in half and place in a saucepan with the sugar, chillies, star anise, bay leaf and water. Simmer very gently for half an hour, diluting with a little cold water if the mixture gets too thick and sticky. Leave to stand for two hours, then add the rum.

Peel the pineapples and slice each one lengthways into four. Cut away the stalky centre and cut each segment into three or four long, thin, rectangular slices. Bathe the slices in the syrup, then lift them out and place on a sheet of foil on a grill tray. Place under a very hot grill for two or three minutes until golden brown, then turn and repeat the process. Serve the pineapple piping hot and anointed with some of the chilli oil, with a portion of the ice cream in a little dish beside it.

WE THINK WE ARE BEING VERY ENGLISH...

when we put fruit in our savoury food. We apologise for eating pork with apple sauce (why? – they were made for each other) or redcurrant jelly with our lamb as though it was a peculiarly English transgression of good taste.

The French used to be especially snobby about this trait, until their own chefs went a bit crazy in the late Seventies and started putting kiwi fruit with their duck and mangoes with their lobster. Somehow the idea of putting duck with orange had a legitimacy that turkey with cranberry sauce lacked.

The more types of cooking I see, the clearer it becomes that the mingling of sweet and sour is a universal habit. Most game in northern Europe is commonly paired with fruit, whether it be reindeer and lingonberries, venison and pears, or pheasant and apples.

In the Mediterranean the Italians have a penchant for the *agro-dolce*: what could be more extraordinary than the Sicilian *caponata*, with a roll call of ingredients as diverse and bizarre as aubergines, celery, pears, sultanas, onions and tomatoes? Even stranger is the Moroccan *pastilla*, made with pigeon, almonds, saffron, coriander, cumin, cinnamon, sugar and filo pastry.

Alongside such strange conjunctions, a little bit of chocolate in a venison sauce seems no more peculiar than, say, a piece of Cheddar cheese with piccalilli.

HALLOWE'EN NIGHT: TRICKS AND TREATS

PUMPKIN SOUP WITH CREAM AND GRUYÈRE

CHARTREUSE OF PARTRIDGE

TARTE TATIN
Serves 6

Like Christmas presents, tomatoes and Coca-Cola, Trick or Treat is something we have to thank the Americans for. It's certainly a very recent import: when I were a lad we were too busy chiselling money out of the local populace for a penny for the guy to be doing any trick-or-treating, even if we had heard of it. Where I live, they still ask for a penny for the guy but it comes more under the category of demanding money with menaces.

Here's a menu of tricks: a soup cooked in a pumpkin, a dish of partridges cooked in a cabbage and an apple tart cooked upside-down. Necessity was the mother of invention in each case. The soup must have been the result of not having a pot:

the whole pumpkin, seeds removed and cavity filled, was perhaps taken along to the baker's bread oven and cooked slowly as the oven cooled, or maybe it was simply stuck in or over the embers of a fire. Whatever its origin, the result is now a sophisticated and elegant production. It's possible the famous tart of the demoiselles Tatin came from some similar improvisation. One can speculate that the sisters had only a pan in which to make their tart but it is more likely that they caramelised the apples in the pan, realised how good they were and had the bright idea of covering them with pastry.

The Chartreuse was an innovation supposedly brought on by the need for deception. The blissful combination of partridge, cabbage and bacon was already well known but it is said that the Carthusian (hence the name) monks craftily hid their meat in or under the cabbage in order to improve their Lenten diet. Thus the story goes, but I find it puzzling. Who were they fooling? Was it their abbot? Unlikely, as the medieval abbot is usually portrayed as a fat cat himself; besides, he would have come up through the ranks and been wise to such a simple trick. Perhaps they thought they could fool their God but that seems theologically naive. Perhaps they had tourists in those days and they were the butt of the deception. My other problem with the story is that I cannot understand what they were doing, eating partridges in Lent in the first place. Game seasons are not just arranged at the whim of the aristocracy for their convenience. Partridges in Lent are mature birds, which means they are a bit tough, and are busy with the business of procreation and should not be disturbed. It would be ecological and gastronomic folly to eat them at that time, in or out of a cabbage.

I can think of few dishes more enjoyable or satisfying to make than these three. They may be an ambitious undertaking in the same menu, especially if they have not been essayed before, but I include them together because they are three of a kind, it's Hallowe'en and they do constitute a balanced menu for the recipient, if not the cook.

PUMPKIN SOUP WITH CREAM AND GRUYÈRE

1 fine pumpkin, weighing 2–3kg
100g Gruyère, or similar, cheese, grated
1 cup of cooked basmati rice
200ml double cream
1 teaspoon ground ginger
¼ teaspoon grated nutmeg

Pumpkins used to be insipid, flavourless things in Britain and I for one could never understand what all the fuss was about. They changed, and my prejudices evaporated. Look for imported varieties with deep orange flesh and a rich but subtle flavour.

The first time I made this soup I didn't use foil and string, and the pumpkin split in the oven: I salvaged the contents and blended the mess into an excellent soup notwithstanding.

Cut a circle in the top of the pumpkin in a 5–7cm radius around the stem. Lift out this 'lid' and proceed to remove all the seeds from inside the pumpkin, scraping them out with a spoon.

Put the cheese, rice, cream and spices in a bowl with a teaspoon of milled white pepper and half a teaspoon of sea salt, mix well and pour into the cavity of the pumpkin. Replace the lid. Wrap the pumpkin in aluminium foil and tie like a parcel with string.

Place the pumpkin in an ovenproof dish and bake in an oven preheated to 200°C / Gas Mark 6 for two hours. Remove from the oven and let stand, still wrapped, in a warm place for ten minutes.

Remove the string and foil and lift off the lid. Using a spoon, very carefully ease the flesh of the pumpkin away from the walls so that it mixes with the rich cream and cheese mixture.

If you have a handheld blender, blend the soup inside the shell to make a smooth purée. If not, simply whisk together the ingredients lightly to produce a more rustic, homespun style of soup. In either event, take the whole pumpkin to the table and ladle out the soup into bowls.

CHARTREUSE OF PARTRIDGE

6 French (red-legged) partridges
100g unsalted butter
Oil
2 Savoy cabbages
500g pancetta or other bacon, in a slab
4 large carrots
1 onion
1 stick of celery
1 glass of dry white wine
2 sprigs of thyme
1 bay leaf
Potato flour or cornflour (optional)

I know grey-leg, or English, partridge are superior in flavour to the red-leg, French variety but this is most definitely a recipe for the latter. The gamy flavour of the English birds would be too strong with the cabbage and they would toughen up badly in the Chartreuse. The French variety is plumper and more tolerant.

Season the partridges very well with salt and pepper. Heat a heavy frying pan and melt a third of the butter in it together with a tablespoon of cooking oil. Brown the partridges in this fat on a steady heat, turning them three ways so that they are evenly coloured. Place the partridges, breast-side up, in a deep roasting tin and roast for eight to ten minutes in an oven preheated to 230°C / Gas Mark 8.

Remove the birds from the oven: they should still be quite pink but feel firm to the touch. Leave to rest for fifteen minutes.

Carefully remove the dark green outer leaves from the cabbages, discarding any wilted or torn ones. Wash the leaves well and then blanch them in plenty of boiling salted water for two or three minutes. They should be tender but still quite firm and very bright green. Drain and then drop into a basin of very cold water to arrest the cooking process and fix the colour. Drain the leaves again and dry them on kitchen paper.

With a long, sharp knife, remove the skin from the bacon. Put the roasting tin in which the partridges were cooked on the stove, melt another third of the butter in it with a little more oil, add the slab of bacon and let it colour slowly.

Peel three of the carrots. Cut the cabbage hearts into quarters, each attached to the central stem. When the bacon has browned nicely, remove it and add the cabbage to the tin. Colour each side of the cabbage well and then return the bacon to the tin, along with the three whole carrots and enough water to submerge the carrots but for the cabbages to be half exposed. Place in a slightly cooler oven (200°C / Gas Mark 6) and braise for an

hour. If the cabbages colour too much or the water evaporates too quickly, cover the tin with aluminium foil.

Cut the onion, celery and remaining carrot into dice about 1cm square. Remove the breasts and legs from the partridges. Chop up the carcasses roughly and brown them in a saucepan in a little oil. Once well coloured, add the chopped vegetables. When they have coloured in turn, add the white wine. Scrape up the residue from the base of the pan with a wooden spoon and add the thyme and bay leaf.

Cover the bones well with cold water (or chicken stock if you have it), bring to the boil and skim very well. Let this stock simmer very gently for one hour.

Take a straight-sided ovenproof dish, about 25cm in diameter and at least 12cm deep. Grease the dish with the remaining butter. Trim away the stalks of the outer leaves of cabbage as much as possible while keeping the leaves perfectly intact. Lay the biggest and best leaf, outer-side down, on the bottom of the dish. Line the dish with the rest of the leaves, making sure they all overlap and there are no gaps. Leave a good overlap all the way around the side of the dish and reserve one big leaf for the final assembly.

Remove the stalks from the braised cabbage hearts and separate the leaves a little. Divide the cabbage into four and place the first quarter in the lined dish, spreading it evenly across the base.

Place the partridge breasts, skin-side down, on top of the cabbage in a pattern like segments of a cake. Cover with another portion of the cabbage. Slice the bacon thickly and lay it across the cabbage in the dish. Add a third portion of the cabbage and then the partridge legs, together with the carrots, thickly sliced. Cover with the remainder of the cabbage and tamp down the whole assembly very well. Place the reserved leaf on top and then bring up the overhanging leaves so that everything is completely enclosed.

Put the Chartreuse in an oven preheated to 220°C / Gas Mark 7 for thirty minutes: it should be very hot in the middle. While it cooks, strain the partridge stock into a pan and simmer until reduced to a gravylike consistency – a very scant teaspoon of potato flour or cornflour may be necessary to thicken it.

Turn the Chartreuse out on to a large plate and take it to the table with the gravy and some plain boiled potatoes.

TARTE TATIN

2 lemons
2kg Cox's apples
125g unsalted butter, slightly softened
125g caster sugar
200g puff pastry

Probably my favourite pudding, to make or to eat. There are Tatins of everything under the sun these days but this was the first and remains the best. A really heavy pan (preferably made of iron or copper), about 22–24cm in diameter, with straight or almost straight sides is pretty well essential for its successful execution.

Cox's are certainly the ideal apple, partly because they have the necessary acidity and depth of flavour to cope with all that sugar and partly because they do not fall apart during cooking.

Squeeze the juice of the lemons and put it in a large pudding basin or similar-shaped bowl with a couple of tablespoons of water. Peel and halve the apples, remove the cores with a teaspoon and roll the halves in the juice.

Smear the butter generously all over the base and sides of the cold pan. Sprinkle the sugar on top and give the pan a shake to ensure it is evenly distributed.

Drain the apples of any lemon juice and arrange them, standing on their sides, in concentric circles, embedding them in the butter / sugar mix. Pack them in as tightly as you can, then put the pan on the fiercest heat you have.

While keeping a beady eye on the pan, roll out the puff pastry into a disc about 2cm wider then the rim of the pan and leave it to rest on a sheet of greaseproof paper on a plate in the fridge. Watch the sides of the pan very closely. You are looking for a good, rich caramel colour to develop. Move the pan around on the heat to ensure the mixture caramelises evenly. It needs a certain courage to keep going in order to get a rich, deep toffee colour. This whole process can take ten to twenty minutes, depending on the pan and the strength of the flame. When it is done, transfer to a heatproof surface or a pot rest.

After five minutes or so, when the pan has cooled a little, drop the disc of pastry on to the apples and let the edges hang over the sides of the pan.

Place the pan in an oven preheated to 220°C / Gas Mark 7 and bake for fifteen minutes, or until the pastry is nicely risen. Remove from the oven and leave to rest for a minute.

The moment of truth has arrived: place an inverted plate, slightly bigger than the pan, over the top. With one hand firmly in place over the plate, grip the handle equally firmly with your other hand and a cloth and, with a determined turn of the wrist, flip the pan over on to the plate. Lower the plate on to a surface, pause a moment and then lift off the pan. Behold, one hopes, a perfect golden circle of apples.

If things are not as perfect as they might be, do not despair, but grab a palette knife and shape the apples into place. This might include a bit of scraping around in the pan, gathering up some residual bits of apple and caramel.

Serve warm, with a bit of double cream.

THERE'S ONLY ONE TARTE TATIN...

(to the tune of 'Juan Camaneira'). Claude Monet used to drive by early motor car sixty miles from Giverny in order to taste the apple tart that the Tatin sisters made in their homespun restaurant in the Sologne. Since that time, one or two other people have learnt to make tarte Tatin and it has become a sacred stone in the repertoire.

The point about this dish is that it is an apple tart. In recent years I have seen pear Tatin, pineapple Tatin and mango Tatin. I have seen shallot, onion and endive Tatins. There is still only one *tarte des demoiselles Tatin*. Only the apple has the sweetness and acidity to complement the flavour of the caramel and the buttery pastry. The rest are all very well but they are, quite simply, not so good.

It's this desperate straining for novelty that betrays so many chefs' efforts. This may not necessarily be the fault of the chef. When cooking becomes fashionable it is inevitable that it falls prey to the vicissitudes of fashion. Lemon tart is good, the chef thinks, but everybody does it, so I'll make it with lime. He doesn't understand that the richness of the egg and cream mix that makes a lemon tart so delicious cries out for the cutting sharpness of lemon and that the fragrant but less strident lime simply does not serve the same purpose.

It is a question of temperament, I suppose. I am not an uninventive cook, in so far as, very occasionally, I have come up with a few new dishes in my time as a chef. It is very satisfying to conceive of something new and original and then have other cooks execute that dish as though it was part of some general repertoire.

Experimentation, however, can be a bit of a hit and miss affair. For pure pleasure, I prefer to cook classic, simple things. There is an alchemy when the simple marriage of lamb with carrots and turnips becomes something as memorable as a navarin d'agneau, or that of butter, sugar, apples and pastry can produce something as transcendental as tarte Tatin.

A VEGETARIAN LUNCH

CREAM OF FENNEL SOUP WITH TAPENADE CROÛTONS

IMAM BAYILDI WITH SPICED SPINACH

AN APPLE AND CHEESE
Serves 6

Just when you thought it safe to go back in the kitchen, they're back. This time, fish is off the menu. One of the reasons we resent the veggie faction is that they are half right. We eat far too much protein. As hunter/gatherers we needed to get as much protein as we could for survival; meat and fish do, after all, constitute the simplest method of ingesting sufficient protein for a balanced diet. The trouble is, we have not learnt to adjust. We are probably getting better, though. After all, fifty years ago, those who could afford it would eat large quantities of protein three times a day, and often meat and fish in the same meal. I'd be much happier eating really good meat or fish occasionally than eating second-rate stuff every day. Our demand for cheap meat gets us into trouble. We should treat the stuff with more respect and be prepared to pay more for it. So it's time to call a truce. I can eat vegetarian food very happily. It's a shame they cannot return the compliment.

We meat-eaters have problems with vegetarian food when it lacks some focal point. Great piles of vegetables on a plate are meaningless to me. It is as though food has to have some identity, or even message, to impart. If a vegetable is to take this central role, it seems to me to make sense not to confuse its message with other messages delivered on the same wavelength, but to exploit its virtues and accentuate its flavour. I cannot imagine a carrot, say, or a piece of broccoli holding down such a part. There are plenty of stronger candidates. The rich fruit-vegetables of late summer, such as tomatoes, peppers and aubergines, all have the depth of flavour coupled with an ability to marry with other flavours. So, too, do the gutsy and lengthy flavours of autumn mushrooms such as ceps, girolles and giant puff balls – these last a revelation, freshly picked, thickly sliced and grilled – all well capable of accommodating strong tastes and seasoning. There are pumpkins, cabbages and Swiss chard in late autumn and winter that also fit the description, and pulses in early summer that qualify, too. Just save us from a plate of vegetables.

A bowl of fruit is a different matter. With the autumn harvest of apples and pears, it often seems silly to try to improve on nature by providing anything else by way of dessert. It is a misconception to think one has to produce three cooked courses in a meal in order to be hospitable. With good cheese and ripe fruit, vegetarians and I are in our respective heavens.

CREAM OF FENNEL SOUP WITH TAPENADE CROÛTONS

1 onion
5 heads of fennel
300g potatoes
50g unsalted butter
500ml milk
50ml double cream or Greek yoghurt
1 tablespoon Pernod or similar
  (optional)

For the tapenade croûtons:

30 black olives, rinsed and stoned
10 anchovy fillets
1 tablespoon capers
1 teaspoon Dijon mustard
Juice of 1 lemon
Olive oil
24 thin slices of baguette, toasted
  under a grill or in the oven

An elegant soup to serve hot now or chilled in summer.

Peel the onion and slice it finely. Pick out the wispy green fronds from the top of the fennel and reserve. Slice the rest finely. Peel the potatoes and cut them into small dice.

Melt the butter in a heavy saucepan and soften the sliced onion in it for three or four minutes, then add the fennel. Season it well, turn the heat down very low and let the fennel slowly collapse for fifteen minutes.

Add the potatoes, then add the milk with an equal volume of water and bring to the boil. Simmer for another twenty-five minutes, by which time the fennel should be tender and the potatoes on the point of disintegrating.

Remove the soup from the stove and blend really well in a liquidiser. Pass through a fine sieve, then pour into a saucepan, bring to the boil and stir in the cream or yoghurt and the Pernod, if using. Finely chop the reserved fennel tops and stir them in too.

For the tapenade, put all the ingredients except the oil and baguette in a liquidiser and blend to a purée. Add a few drops of olive oil to help blend the mass to a smooth paste. Smear a thin coating of the tapenade on each croûton.

Check the seasoning of the soup and serve piping hot. Serve the tapenade croûtons on the side, to dip or float in the soup as desired.

IMAM BAYILDI

6 medium-sized aubergines
Olive oil
1 large onion
6 cloves of garlic
4 chopped tinned tomatoes
1 teaspoon sugar
½ bunch of flat-leaf parsley
Lemon wedges and Greek yoghurt, to serve

The translation is "the priest swooned". It was the melting texture of the aubergine that caused the swoon and I think it is worth playing this absolutely straight, with no extra flourishes. Experimentalists can certainly play around to good effect with cumin, cayenne and coriander, for example, in the stuffing.

This should be eaten Turkish style: lukewarm and in a leisurely fashion.

Peel alternate strips lengthwise off each aubergine. Put the aubergines in a colander, sprinkle with a tablespoon of sea salt and leave for thirty minutes. Then wipe clean with a paper towel and fry in plenty of olive oil, browning on all sides.

Peel the onion and garlic and chop them finely. Make a sauce by stewing the onion and garlic in olive oil until soft, then adding the chopped tomatoes, sugar and some salt and pepper. Cook gently until thick. Wash and chop the parsley, add it to the sauce and then remove from the heat.

Lay the aubergines in a gratin dish. Cut a big slash down through each one, taking care not to reach the bottom or to cut through the sides. Open out the pocket, cram with the sauce mixture and then close up the pouch as much as possible. Pour a cup of water into the dish and sprinkle some olive oil over the top of the aubergines. Cover with foil and bake for an hour in an oven preheated to 200°C / Gas Mark 6. Check to make sure the aubergines are perfectly tender throughout.

Serve the aubergines with the lemon wedges, a scoop of Greek yoghurt, the Spiced spinach and a rice pilaff (see page 79).

SPICED SPINACH

1 teaspoon cumin seeds
½ teaspoon coriander seeds
Seeds from 3 cardamom pods
1kg fresh spinach
Oil
75g unsalted butter
1 clove of garlic, peeled and chopped
½ teaspoon finely chopped fresh root
  ginger
A pinch of freshly grated nutmeg

I have often heard it said that spinach should be cooked in very little water. That strikes me as disastrous advice, as it allows the spinach to stew. I like to cook it either in a great deal of water and then squeeze it dry or, more often, in no water at all.

Toast the seeds in a dry pan over a high heat, turning them regularly and taking care they do not burn. Put them in a grinder or spice mill and grind finely.

Wash the spinach in several changes of water and dry well. Heat a film of cooking oil in a large pan until it gets very hot. Add the spinach in one go and leave for one minute. Turn the spinach completely over until it has collapsed but the leaves are still bright green and firm.

Drain immediately in a colander, pressing down to force all the liquid out of the spinach.

Melt the butter in a large pan, add the garlic and ginger and cook very gently, on no account allowing them to burn.

Add the spices and continue to cook them extremely softly. When the spices have formed a kind of paste, add the spinach and turn it in this mixture until it is tender.

AN APPLE AND CHEESE

I like to finish a meal at leisure. I do not have much of a sweet tooth. I would always eat a pudding if someone had made it for me but would only order one in a restaurant out of a sense of professional curiosity.

I like my cheese and I like a bit of fruit. I can nibble away at a morsel of Roquefort, I adore a spoonful of truly runny Vacherin Mont d'Or and there is nothing to match the splendour of a great, oozing wedge of Brie. As the Monty Python character said, "J'adore les beaux fromages de France." But after a light meal I might hanker after something a little more substantial, a more lingering way to finish. Then a piece of fruit, an apple or pear, and a hunk of hard cheese is the only way to go.

A ripe pear and a piece of crystalline Parmesan is a glorious example, but so too is a Russet apple with a mature Caerphilly or a Cox's Orange Pippin with a really good farmhouse Cheddar. I like to quarter my apple with a sharp paring knife, scoop out the core and pare away the skin.

A nibble of cheese followed by a crunch of apple and you have one of those perfect marriages one hears about.

WHY DO PEOPLE BOTHER TO MAKE FRESH PASTA?

The mystery, to me, is why anybody bothers at all, since the results are usually so dire. Good pasta, like bread, is so simple in its composition that the quality of the ingredients is paramount. Serious pasta makers find themselves importing not just the flour from Italy (Tipo 00, a hard and strong flour especially made for the purpose) but the eggs as well.

In the right hands, there is no doubt that fresh pasta can be superb, especially if it has been prepared by hand, if not that day, then the night before. After a superb dinner in a Piedmont restaurant once, I wandered into the kitchen to congratulate the chef, only to find the whole family – his wife, her two sisters, his mother-in-law and his brother – helping to make the agnolotti for the next day. Even for the experts, it is an extremely labour-intensive business.

In this country the trouble is the packet stuff is usually much better. It's made by people who know what they are doing. If you don't think the stuff you are buying is particularly good, shop around and buy an Italian brand. It seems silly to waste time making an inferior product – convenient food is not, after all, the same thing as convenience food.

INTERLUDE

PASTA

Who would have thought how much we would come to rely on pasta? For quick lunches, children's meals, lazy suppers and smart dinners, it has come to rival bread and potatoes as our favourite starch.

I will not bother you with detailed directions on cooking techniques or, to what degree it should be cooked. I suggest plenty of well-salted water at a rolling boil, and take a bit out to check one minute before you think it is cooked. Oh, and do not drain it too thoroughly, as it will simply get dry and sticky.

FETTUCCINE WITH MUSSELS

2kg mussels
1 glass of white wine
4 plum tomatoes
A sprig of thyme
4 shallots
2 cloves of garlic
Olive oil
200ml double cream
500g fettuccine (or tagliatelle or other
*   ribbon-type pasta)*
Serves 4–6

The smaller, bouchot-type mussels are especially good for this.

Wash the mussels, then steam them open in the white wine as described in Mussel soup (see page 138). Shell them, reserving the cooking juices.

Peel the tomatoes by blanching them in boiling water and slipping off the skins. Remove all the seeds and chop the flesh into small, neat dice. Save the skins, juice and seeds for the sauce. Sprinkle the diced tomato with the leaves of the thyme and some salt.

Peel the shallots and garlic, chop them quite finely and stew in a little olive oil. Add the tomato waste and strain the cooking liquid from the mussels on to this base.

Boil vigorously until there is barely a cup of liquid left, then whisk in the double cream and some milled pepper. Simmer this gently until it is quite thick and then strain into another saucepan. Add the shelled mussels and the tomato dice.

Bring a large pot of water to a rolling boil with plenty of salt. Cook the pasta in this and drain when it is still al dente. Return t quickly to the pan, add the mussels and their delicious sauce, turn very carefully so that they are well distributed and serve.

TAGLIATELLE AL RAGÙ

50g pancetta
200g shin of beef
200g luganega sausage
1 onion
1 carrot
1 stick of celery
2 cloves of garlic
2 tablespoons olive oil
2 tablespoons tomato purée
250ml dry red wine
250ml chicken stock
2 bay leaves
A pinch of grated nutmeg
100ml milk
500g tagliatelle verde
Freshly grated Parmesan cheese
Serves 4–6

Proper ragù is a lot more effort than chucking some mince in a pan with some tinned tomatoes, but the result is a world apart. Spag bol may never be the same again.

If you do not have a mincer or a compliant butcher, cut the meat into small pieces and then chop it in a food processor with a finger on the pulse button. Mince the pancetta and the beef separately.

Remove the meat from the sausage skins. Chop up all the vegetables and the garlic extremely finely.

Heat the olive oil in a heavy saucepan, add the minced pancetta and cook on a medium heat for five minutes, stirring occasionally.

Add the chopped vegetables and soften over a gentle heat for ten minutes. Turn up the heat and add the minced beef and the sausage meat. Season well with salt and milled black pepper. Stir and turn constantly as you seal the meat on every side.

Once it is sealed, add the tomato purée and mix very well before adding the red wine, stock, bay leaves and nutmeg. Bring the mixture to the boil and proceed to simmer for at least two hours. It will need little attention as it bubbles away quietly at the back of the stove. The liquid should gradually reduce until the sauce is rich and syrupy and needs diluting a little with the milk towards the end of the cooking time. You should now have a soft, rich and unguent sauce.

Bring a large pot of water with a teaspoon of salt to a rolling boil. Drop in the tagliatelle and cook until al dente – still firm but no longer hard in the middle.

Drain immediately in a colander, saving a little of the cooking water, and then return the pasta to the pot, adding the sauce. Turn together, adding a little of the water to achieve a thorough coating of sauce on the pasta.

Serve immediately, with plenty of freshly grated Parmesan.

SPAGHETTI WITH CRAB, GARLIC AND CHILLI

500g spaghetti
200g cooked brown crab meat
Juice of 1 lemon
50g butter, melted
2 cloves of garlic
¼ red chilli
1 tablespoon olive oil
6 basil leaves
Serves 4–6

Bring a large pot of salted water to a rolling boil and push in the spaghetti, using the circumference of the pan to twist all the pasta in. As soon as it softens, separate the strands with a fork and let it cook at a vigorous simmer for eight or nine minutes.

Place the brown crab meat in a blender. Season well with salt, black pepper and the lemon juice. Liquidise, adding the melted butter as you go.

Chop the garlic and chilli very finely. Just before the pasta is cooked, heat the olive oil in a large saucepan and stew the garlic and chilli until they are translucent. When the pasta is cooked to your liking, drain it lightly and add to the garlic and chilli mixture. Do not let the pasta get too dry, a little of the cooking water should be allowed to remain with it to help emulsify the sauce.

Turn the pasta in the garlic and chilli oil and then add the crab meat mixture, which should have a creamy consistency. Using a wooden fork, turn the pasta really thoroughly, adding a little extra pasta cooking water if the dish is too dry. Chop the basil coarsely and sprinkle it into the pasta. Taste for seasoning and serve. Do not be tempted to offer any cheese with it.

PENNE WITH BROCCOLI, GARLIC AND ANCHOVIES

1 red pepper
4 cloves of garlic
6 anchovies
500g broccoli
500g penne rigate
100ml virgin olive oil
Serves 4–6

Sear the red pepper under a hot grill until the skin blisters, then transfer it to a plastic bag, seal and leave for ten minutes. Remove from the bag, peel off the skin and remove any seeds from the pepper. Cut it into thin julienne strips about 4cm in length.

Peel the garlic and chop it finely. Drain the anchovies of their oil and chop them finely also.

Cut the broccoli into small florets the size of a walnut. Peel the thicker stalks and cut them into 2cm lengths. Bring a large pot of well salted water to a rolling boil and blanch the broccoli in it for two minutes. Remove the broccoli and refresh in cold water, then drain.

Bring the same water back to a rolling boil and add the penne. Stir well and continue to boil, not too vigorously, for nine minutes or until the pasta is cooked but still al dente.

Meanwhile, heat the olive oil in a saucepan, add the anchovies and garlic and stew gently for a couple of minutes. Add the sliced pepper and the broccoli and stew for five minutes, turning frequently. Drain the pasta and add it immediately to the broccoli mixture. Turn together well, check the seasoning and serve.

WINTER

DINNER FOR TWO

FOOTBALLERS' LUNCH

THE DINNER PARTY

BOXING DAY LUNCH

THE VEGETARIAN IN LENT

WINTER

On the face of it, as winter drags on, times get worse for the cook. The vegetables certainly become a bit monotonous, the supply of potatoes deteriorates as we wait for the first new potatoes from Jersey and the only homegrown fruits are apples and pears from the cold store. Even the game season dries up, with no feathered game after January.

Life could be grim. A browse through the winter menu of May Little's *A Year's Dinners*, my guide to the eating habits of a bygone age of Edwardian respectability, when every middle-class home could boast a couple of servants and every meal at least three courses, can be a dispiriting experience. One learns the true meaning of austerity. A Lenten menu of boiled cod on Fridays, grey fricassees, brown Windsor soup and the dreaded mulligatawny on Mondays reminds me

of the worst excesses of school food. Fridays were always feared at my prep school. It was not fish. Friday's supper was matron's night off and the 'principal' of the school – in fact the owner, an old harridan with piercing blue eyes and a basilisk stare – presided. It was the 'savoury spaghetti' that we dreaded most, fat, greasy pasta punctuated by lumps of gristle, and the knowledge that we were not allowed to leave the table without a clean plate. We traded plastic bags that we could smuggle in and use to dispose of the dreaded spaghetti in our pockets. It is worth remembering just how ghastly the good old days really were.

Fish was in no better supply then than it is now. Scallops, mussels, Dublin Bay prawns, wild trout and salmon are at their best in those cold months of late winter but they could have been on the moon for all the local fishmonger knew about it. It was ever thus: good fishmongers were as few and far between then as now. It is a strange anomaly, and a sad reminder of our gastronomic oafishness, to see the way that we, as a maritime nation, turn our backs on the sea and look for excitement in the novelty of the latest craze, whether it be Moroccan, Mexican or so-called Mediterranean food.

In these days of refrigerated transport it is even harder to understand our apathy towards fish. Two of the best seafood meals I have ever eaten were in Madrid and Paris, where I consumed molluscs and fish of a sweetness and freshness that seems unthinkable so far from the sea. Put simply, the people of these countries care more, demand quality, and get it. They are prepared to pay for it, too. Here, we would rather spend the money on a Nintendo game for the children than teach them how to get every morsel of sweet flesh out of a langoustine, or prise a periwinkle from its shell.

Midwinter is a time of bounty in some respects. Long before Christianity, Europeans used to raid the store cupboard of hams, fattened geese, salt beef, dried beans and fruit at the time we now celebrate Christmas. It was too expensive to fatten animals over winter, so they were killed and their meat salted to preserve it, but poultry could live off kitchen scraps and loose grain throughout the year, and there was always game in some form. Venison, hare and wild boar would go to the rich man's table, rabbits to the poor: not much has changed, except that only the rich are now prepared to eat rabbit – put it on in the local pub and see where that gets you.

DINNER FOR TWO

GRIDDLED SCALLOPS WITH PEA PURÉE AND MINT VINAIGRETTE

BRAISED PHEASANT WITH CREAM AND PIMENTON AND SALSIFY

BAKED QUINCES WITH CINNAMON AND VIN SANTO

Serves 2

However much one cooks at home, whether entertaining or catering for a large family, we still, more often than not, find ourselves cooking for only one or two at the end of the day. There may be a brief time when teenagers are prepared to sit down and eat proper food before they fly the nest and make their own gastronomic discoveries, but the age of the sit-down family meal seems to be over, for better or worse. There is a notion that family unity was cemented on these occasions but I daresay as many families disintegrated over a traumatic Sunday lunch as were ever harmonised by the experience.

Cooking for two is the most natural and relaxed sort of work. It does not involve the sheer labour that comes with volume, nor the logistics required. If you are cooking for two, you are on home ground, cooking favoured ingredients and employing much-loved equipment that has seen it all before. My own collection includes the little ridged griddle pan that accommodates two sirloin steaks or six lamb chops to perfection, an old copper sauté pan in which I have fricasseed countless chickens and sautéed veal kidneys and pork fillets, and an oval frying pan that allows two soles to nudge neatly together. And then there is the little orange Le Creuset casserole.

Every time I see one of these small, oval casserole dishes I have a wistful urge to cook a chicken or some smaller bird. This is hardly suitable for restaurant practice. In restaurants we cook six or ten birds at a time and make our sauce separately from stock, trimmings and vegetables. The whole cooking process is dissected and divided into component parts, ready for quick reassembly at the customer's command. The jus and the roast chicken that you see on your plate have probably only just been introduced, and the jus was probably made from a different bird altogether. This is cheating of a kind but not necessarily the worse for that. A friend of mine told me about a chicken dish he had at Taillevent, one of the grandest restaurants in Paris and the longest holder of three stars in the Michelin guide. He purred with pleasure as he described this poulet de Bresse en cocotte that arrived at the table in its little copper casserole, the lid sealed on by a piece of disposable pastry, thus ensuring the juices could not escape. It struck me that he had paid a fortune to eat a dish, albeit made with an extremely expensive chicken, that had been untouched by human hand. Often, when one sees what the very best restaurants do, one realises that it is usually very little: the skill is more in the buying and the serving – the best ingredients, after all, need the least interference.

My pot-roast pheasant is a little more complicated than that simple poulet en cocotte. Pheasant, after all, needs a little mollycoddling if it is not to be tough. Much as I adore the classic English treatment of game birds, just roasted with a little bacon and served with bread sauce and game chips, only a young, but well hung, pheasant will remain tender and not dry up under such simple treatment.

It is sad that quinces are so hard to find in this country. I adore their fragrance and their rich, deep flavour. They say the way to sell a house is to impregnate it with the smell of fresh roasted coffee or freshly baked bread. I think the pervasive perfume of quinces baking in the oven, slowly becoming more and more aromatic as they gradually change from a dull yellow to a deep pink, is even more enticing. A bit like mirabelles, if you see any it is worth buying the lot as not only do they keep well but they make a multitude of preserves.

Here, then, is an elaborate menu for two. I do not suppose anyone is going to cook all three dishes for the same meal but there is no reason why not. Once mastered, they are all relatively quick to prepare and it is a reasonably balanced menu. However, any one of them would be a treat.

GRIDDLED SCALLOPS WITH PEA PURÉE AND MINT VINAIGRETTE

2 spring onions
Butter
The outside leaves of a lettuce
150g fresh shelled or frozen peas
1 bunch of mint
Nutmeg Sugar
½ glass of white wine
75ml double cream
Lemon juice
50ml cider vinegar or white wine
  vinegar
125ml sunflower oil
8 scallops, shucked, rinsed and cut in
  half if very large

Although you will not need so much mint vinaigrette, it is difficult to make in smaller quantity and keeps well in the fridge, to accompany some lamb chops on another occasion.

To make the purée, slice the spring onions and stew them in a little butter. Finely shred the lettuce leaves and add to the pan, then stir in the peas. Add three or four leaves of mint, a small pinch of nutmeg, a good pinch of sugar and some salt and pepper.

Add the white wine and then stew, covered, on a low heat for half an hour. When the peas are very tender and swollen, add the cream and simmer briskly to reduce, until it is in danger of catching on the sides of the pan.

Remove from the heat and purée in a blender until very smooth. Sharpen the seasoning with a little squeeze of lemon and more salt and pepper if it needs it. Put the purée in a small saucepan and keep warm.

To make the vinaigrette, pick six or seven sprigs of mint, chop the leaves very roughly and put them in a blender. Add a teaspoon of sugar and a big pinch of salt. Bring the vinegar up to the boil and pour over the mint. Switch on the blender and add the oil in a steady trickle. Check the seasoning and adjust with lemon, salt and pepper, if necessary.

To cook the scallops, salt them lightly, leave for ten minutes and then pat them dry with kitchen paper. Lightly brush them with a little sunflower oil.

Get a heavy, dry frying pan or a griddle very hot and put the scallops in it in one by one. Do not move them for a couple of minutes but let them brown well.

Turn and cook for another two minutes, then remove. They should be just hot in the middle, but very moist.

To serve, arrange the scallops around a mound of the pea purée on each plate and drizzle the vinaigrette between them. Do not drown the scallops.

BRAISED PHEASANT WITH CREAM AND PIMENTON

1 plump pheasant
25g butter, plus a teaspoon
2 shallots
2 cloves of garlic
1 teaspoon pimenton
1 small glass of dry vermouth or dry
*   white wine*
150ml double cream

"Don't ever ask a Hungarian food expert to tell you about paprika unless you are prepared to hear more about the subject than you want to know," testily wrote Elizabeth David, but I expect the Spanish might be equally obsessive about pimenton, which is very similar to paprika. It comes in very nice little tins, goes off quicker than one would like and is utterly and distinctively Spanish.

Season the trussed pheasant well with salt and pepper. Heat an ovenproof casserole just large enough to hold the bird and melt the 25g butter in it. Add the pheasant, on its side, and then turn down the heat so the butter foams gently without burning. Leave the pheasant on its side so that it colours really well, then turn it on its other side and repeat the process, finishing with the bird on its back. The whole process should take about ten minutes.

Remove the bird from the casserole and discard the butter. Do not clean the casserole.

Peel the shallots and garlic and chop them extremely finely. Melt the teaspoon of butter in the casserole and add the shallots and garlic. Sweat them very gently so that they become translucent and take no colour.

Add the pimenton and stir it in very well, scraping up the juices from the base of the dish as you go. After a moment or two, add the vermouth or white wine and let it simmer while you finish off the job of deglazing, or collecting up all the juices that have caramelised on the base of the casserole.

Do not let the wine reduce too much. Pour in the double cream and bring it briefly to the boil, no more, before returning the pheasant to the dish. Cover with a lid or a well-fitting piece of foil and place in an oven preheated to 200°C / Gas Mark 6 for fifteen minutes.

Remove the casserole from the oven and leave to stand, still covered, for ten minutes. Then lift out the pheasant and place it on a chopping board. Once it is cool enough to handle, carefully remove the legs, taking care to get the 'oyster' that lies under the backbone at the very top corner of the leg. Then slice down either side of the breastbone and remove the breasts, together with the wings. The breasts should be just cooked through, and the underside of the thighs still slightly bloody.

Put the casserole back on the heat. If the creamy sauce is very runny, bring it back to the boil and simmer it over a medium to high heat (it should not bubble up uncontrollably) for a few moments until it thickens.

Add the legs and poach them in this creamy sauce for a couple of minutes, just enough to allow the meat to cook through. Now add the breasts and gently heat them through. On no account let the meat boil in the sauce or cook too long, as it will toughen very quickly. The sauce may need a little pinch of salt and a squeeze of lemon to sharpen it up.

Serve immediately, with some rice pilaff (see page 79) and salsify.

SALSIFY

400g salsify (or scorzonera)
4 tablespoons white wine vinegar
50g butter
Juice of 1/2 lemon
1 dessertspoon finely chopped
  parsley

There is a lot of fuss talked about cooking salsify, and elaborate methods of avoiding discoloration advocated, but I have always found the vinegar trick works very well, as long as they are not actually cooked in the vinegar.

Place the salsify in a sink of cold water and scrub off the dirt. Drain them well. Place each stick on a board and peel it in long strips away from you, swiveling the vegetable with your other hand as you peel. Cut each stick into three fingerlength pieces as you go, placing them immediately in the vinegar in a bowl, turning them each time.

Bring a large pot of well salted water to the boil. Drain the salsify of the vinegar very thoroughly in a colander and then plunge them immediately into the boiling water. Cook at a steady simmer for twelve to fifteen minutes, or until they are tender and give no resistance to a small insertion with a knife. Drain them immediately. The salsify can be left to cool at this point or finished straight away.

To finish, heat the butter in a small frying pan and add the salsify when it is gently foaming. Season the salsify well and let them colour a soft gold. Turn up the heat, add the lemon juice and chopped parsley, roll the salsify well in this mixture and then serve.

BAKED QUINCES WITH CINNAMON AND VIN SANTO

1 lemon
6 quinces
150ml Vin Santo or other sweet wine
1 cinnamon stick
6 cloves
75g caster sugar

The Vin Santo is hardly essential, although it does produce the most luscious liquor. You could substitute almost any sweet wine, or even the unwanted sweet sherry which has been in the cupboard since the Christmas before last.

With a potato peeler, take off the zest of the lemon in broad strips. Cut the lemon in quarters.

Cut the quinces in quarters, then cut away the cores (you may want to keep them for jam or jelly) and rub the pieces with the lemon. Place the quarters, skin-side down, in an enamelled iron or earthenware dish that will hold all the quinces in one layer.

Pour the wine over the fruit and distribute the lemon zest, cinnamon and cloves around. Sprinkle the sugar over the quinces and bake in an oven preheated to 170°C / Gas Mark 3 for about two hours. The fruit should turn a beautiful rusty pink and be very tender.

Serve cold with some unsweetened whipped cream, or mascarpone or crème fraîche and perhaps some Biscotti (see page 152).

THE SCALLOPS WITH PEA PURÉE AND MINT VINAIGRETTE...

is what is known as a signature dish. Customers coming to the restaurant expect to see it on the menu, along with one or two other dishes (griddled foie gras with a sweetcorn pancake; chicken and goat's cheese mousse with olives), and would probably continue to order it even if I had the audacity to take it off.

I am perfectly happy to leave it on for many reasons. To come up with an original dish and a new combination of flavours is rare enough. Most of the time all we chefs do is either rework old combinations or invent bizarre and inappropriate conjunctions.

Some of the greatest chefs have put little prize on originality but seen themselves as perpetrators of a great tradition, with their job being to defend standards and maintain authenticity. Such an approach may seem hidebound – chefs are, in the main, fiercely conservative – but a rigorous insistence on high standards, on doing things the way they were always done, has ensured the survival of all great cuisines, whether Japanese, Chinese, Italian or French.

I enjoy conservatism in restaurants. I love to go to an Italian restaurant that displays its antipasti, makes its pasta by hand and grills the fish or meat simply with no adornment: these are people who know what they are doing and trust their ingredients.

My scallop dish is a clever conjunction of flavours but what makes it special is our delivery, five times a week, of live scallops from the west coast of Scotland. They are deliciously sweet and meaty, and it was these attributes that made me compare scallops to lamb and wonder if a sweet and vinegary mint sauce would do the same job for the mollusc that it did for the meat. The purée has some of the same sweetness and is a nice contrast in texture. But it is the scallops that dazzle.

FOOTBALLERS' LUNCH

LE CASSOULET
Serves about 12

There are some dishes that one never tires of cooking. Although it is probably also true that one never tires of eating them either, it is not quite the same thing. Cooking and eating are different sports, which do not necessarily meet in some kind of neat binary opposition.

The ultimate pleasure in cooking, of course, lies in giving pleasure to others, but it has to said there is an awful lot of solipsistic enjoyment to be had along the way. Take cassoulet. Everybody loves it and no other dish lends itself to second and third helpings so easily. And yet, truth be told, for the serious cook, there is always a niggle. No cassoulet is ever quite as good as the cassoulet one has made oneself, and even that will be flawed in some trifling but tragic fashion. The perfect cassoulet is always performing a disappearing act: it is like the great American novel or the great white whale of gastronomy.

Cassoulet, like Gaul, is supposedly divided into three parts, or styles, those of Carcassonne, Castelnaudary and Toulouse, but in truth there are more cassoulets than there are cooks. I have made the dish countless times but no two have ever been remotely the same. Like many cooks before me, however, I am a cassoulet obsessive: the slightest flavour out of kilter, the tiniest predominance of one ingredient not entirely in accordance with my whim of the moment and I am thrown into despair, resolving to make a cassoulet again, and soon.

The only problem is that cassoulet is hardly an everyday thing to prepare. This is not because it is particularly difficult or arduous. Many people are put off attempting cassoulet because it "takes three days to make it". If you count one day for soaking the beans it does indeed take three days, but ninety-nine per cent of that time can be spent sleeping, surfing the web or reading the papers whilst the cassoulet gurgles away very quietly on the back of the stove or in the oven.

It is not difficulty that deters, but volume. The fascination of cassoulet lies in its variety of meats (there is hardly a vegetable interest, after all) and it is just not feasible to make a small cassoulet. Perfectly decent dishes of pork and beans can be made on a small scale but they cannot be cassoulet. It is a dish for the big occasion.

The endless arguments that occupy cassoulet obsessives all centre on the selection of meats for inclusion in what should be an unglazed earthenware pot (a *cassol d'Issel*, to be ridiculously precise). Pork rinds, cut into little squares and cooked with the beans until they practically melt, are a constant in almost every recipe, as is preserved goose. This latter is expensive and increasingly obscure. All but diehard traditionalists now substitute duck, since it is considerably more economical than its elder and noisier brother. After these two, it becomes a bit of a free-for-all: sausages, yes, but a big garlic sausage, several Toulouse sausages or what? A friend of mine uses Polish boiling sausages and I favour the little Italian luganega on the grounds of availability and their lean, meaty consistency.

Most people use some kind of pork but there are disputes as to whether it should be fresh or salted. The fights really start when it comes to lamb or mutton. There is no doubt that the purist view eschews the sheep. The possibly original Castelnaudary version has none, but in Carcassonne half a leg of lamb is de rigueur. As usual, I side with the revisionists, but suspect that an authentic cassoulet would probably include the richer flavour of mutton rather than the sacrifice of young lamb to what is, after all, a peasant stew, however glorious.

If this minefield of obsessional disputes makes the reader a little fearful of even attempting the dish, there is a reward for the diligence involved. People adore cassoulet. Whatever its defects for the purists, even they will be in the queue for more.

This recipe will happily feed twelve. As to the footballers, we are not talking about athletes here, but a good cassoulet will keep you well insulated for an afternoon on the terraces.

LE CASSOULET

The duck:

6 duck legs
500g rock salt
1 dessertspoon milled black pepper
6 cloves of garlic
A few sprigs of thyme
3 bay leaves
1 glass of dry white wine
250g duck fat, if available, or 100ml
  sunflower oil

Do not trim any of the fat from the duck legs. Place a layer of rock salt in a flat dish. Rub the lean part of the duck legs with the pepper and lay the legs, skin-side up, on top of the salt. Peel the garlic and place between the pieces of duck, together with the thyme and bay leaves. Cover the duck completely with the rest of the salt. Cover with clingfilm or foil and refrigerate for thirty-six hours.

Lift the duck legs out of their resultant brine. Save the garlic, thyme and bay leaves to cook with the beans. Place the duck legs in a casserole with the white wine, duck fat or oil and a cup of water. Cover with a tight-fitting lid and place in an oven preheated to 150°C / Gas Mark 2 for three hours. The duck will render out its fat and should poach very gently without boiling. When it is cooked it should be meltingly tender but should not quite fall off the bone. Leave to cool in its fat.

The beans:

1.5kg long white haricot beans
4 salted pig's trotters
500g salted or smoked streaky bacon,
  in a slab
100g pork rind, cut into small squares
2 carrots
1 onion
6 cloves
A generous sprig of parsley

Any long, round, white bean will work: the Italian cannellini beans, though a little small, make a good cassoulet. Care in their treatment is more important than the exact choice of bean. When cooked properly, they should be plump and very tender, their skins soft but unbroken.

If you cannot face pig's trotters, a piece of salted pork shoulder will be leaner and less gelatinous.

Wash the beans in plenty of cold water, taking care to pick out any stones or dirt. Put the beans in a large pot with three times their volume of cold water, cover and leave to soak for at least twelve hours.

Drain the beans and rinse them well. Place in a large casserole and cover with cold water again. Bring gently to a full boil and then drain. Place the trotters and bacon in another large pot of cold water and bring slowly to the boil. Pour away this water in turn as soon as it boils. Combine the beans with the trotters, bacon and pork rind in the biggest casserole available.

Peel the carrots but leave them whole. Peel the onion and stud it with the cloves. Add the carrots and onion to the pot, with the parsley sprig and the garlic and herbs from salting the duck. Add enough water to cover everything generously. Bring gently to the boil and very carefully skim off any scum that comes to the surface. Cook the beans on the gentlest possible simmer on top of the stove for about three hours, until they are very soft but not breaking up. Very old or large beans may take longer.

The lamb:

3–4kg shoulder of mature lamb or
  hogget, on the bone
2 onions
4 overripe or tinned plum tomatoes
1 glass of dry white wine

If you like the taste of mutton and can get it, by all means use mutton.

Heat some of the duck fat from the first stage in a roasting dish. Pepper and lightly salt the lamb and then brown it well on all sides in the duck fat. Peel the onions, cut them into slices 1cm thick and lay these underneath the meat. Transfer to an oven preheated to 220°C / Gas Mark 7 and roast for half an hour, then add the tomatoes to the roasting dish. After another twenty minutes, pour the white wine over the meat and continue cooking for another half an hour. The meat should be well done but have rendered a syrupy, caramelised juice in the tray. Lift out the meat and pour 500ml of cold water into the tin, scraping up any coagulated residue. Bring this juice to the boil and then strain into a bowl. Let stand for half an hour, then skim off any fat from the surface.

The sausages and assembly:

1kg luganega
750g whole garlic sausage
250g breadcrumbs

Place the sausages in an oiled frying pan (in a coil if they are unlinked) and brown gently on top of the stove for a few moments, then transfer to an oven preheated to 220°C / Gas Mark 7 (you can put them in with the lamb) and cook for another ten minutes.

Lift the duck pieces out of their fat, place on a roasting tray and brown in the oven at 230°C / Gas Mark 8 for ten minutes. Leave to cool for ten minutes and then cut in half through the knee joint. Remove the lamb from the bone and cut into small chunks about 4cm square and 1cm thick. Cut the bacon slab into 3cm cubes. Remove any meat from the trotters and cut into similarsized pieces. Cut the luganega into 3cm lengths.

Remove the carrots, onion and herbs from the beans, which should be just covered by their cooking liquid. Add all the cut meat to the beans, along with the juice from roasting the lamb. Pour this ensemble into a deep casserole and sprinkle over half the breadcrumbs. Drizzle a little of the duck fat over these and place the casserole in an oven preheated to 220°C / Gas Mark 7 for half an hour.

Remove from the oven, break the crust that should have formed and stir it into the cassoulet. Moisten with a little cold water if the juices are getting too thick and drying out. Lay thick slices of the garlic sausage on top of the cassoulet and then repeat the breadcrumb and duck fat crust. Return to the oven for twenty minutes before serving.

Serve nothing before the cassoulet, a green salad with it and a very light dessert afterwards. This is serious fare.

INSTEAD OF SOAKING THE BEANS...

an alternative method of preparing them is to wash them carefully as before, then cover with three times their volume of cold water and bring to the boil. Remove the beans from the stove, cover the pot with a lid and leave to stand for threequarters of an hour. Throw away this pernicious and flatulenceinducing liquid (Elizabeth David says that Languedoc housewives bottle it as a stain remover, but this might be going to extremes). Proceed as before, with fresh water, the bacon and aromatics.

Mention beans to an Englishman and you invite ribald jokes about flatulence. Jerusalem artichokes invoke the same reaction. "Beans, beans, a marvellous fruit / The more you eat the more you toot", runs the rhyme, and it is true that ill-prepared beans can cause an explosive reaction.

The Tuscans are renowned for their bean-eating but there is no petomanic snigger attached to this reputation. Properly cooked, beans should be innocent of the charge, and our derision is testimony to gastronomic incompetence. Jerusalem artichokes, on the other hand, are less easy to defend. Apparently they were eaten a great deal during the war, in which case it cannot have been very pleasant in those air-raid shelters.

THE DINNER PARTY

MUSSEL SOUP

COD WITH PARSLEY SAUCE

LEMON TART

Serves 6

The secret of a dinner party, as most people know, is to avoid undue stress and to give oneself time to talk to one's guests before dinner. This is easier said than done, in my experience. There are some rules that are worth following. If you do not know the people, then know the food and do stuff you love. The idea is to give people a good time and not to try and show off. Exhibitionism in cooking is undoubtedly the curse of our times. The desperate need to be different and original, exemplified by most television cooking, stands in the way of the proper appreciation of good food.

I acted as a judge on *Masterchef*, the longest-running television cookery programme at the moment of writing. Just the once, you understand, and I would like to claim that I turned down subsequent offers to reappear but some note of diffidence in my demeanour must have communicated itself both to the producers and the greater audience, for no such invitation was forthcoming.

I had heard beforehand the acrimony that was heaped upon Sir Terence Conran after he had appeared on the programme. He had dared to criticise the food and had seemed ungracious in commenting on the lack of seasoning and the inanity of some of the ideas. I was determined to avoid the same mistake and resolved to maintain a mask of benignity and be the soul of encouragement. It was the liver that was my undoing. One very nice bloke, a well-fed-looking professional man with an absolute passion for cooking, came up with a menu of seared tuna with ginger and soy, calf's liver with pineapple and a chocolate bread and butter pudding to finish. I could not help myself looking askance at the liver and pineapple and mumbling that "the jury was still out" on the question of their compatibility. After the raw tuna, the liver had been a bit of a challenge in the first place, and the pineapple was definitely a leap too far, to my mind. As to the dessert, I adore bread and butter pudding and I love chocolate but I would as much want to put them together as I would – and I hesitate here, since most outlandish couplings get tried sooner or later – chocolate with sardines.

Give them cod. Ten or fifteen years ago it would have been daringly *nouveau pauvre* to offer cod but we have come to look with new eyes on that once plentiful fish. Mark Kurlansky's brilliant book on the subject demonstrates the importance of the cod trade in both European and American culture but also promotes a respect for its value.

Cod is following the path of oysters and the opposite course to salmon. Once hugely plentiful and the food of the poor, both oysters and cod have become less plentiful and therefore more highly esteemed. If cod really becomes as threatened a species as pessimistic forecasts predict, you can guarantee its price will rival that of turbot. In the meantime, enjoy it. Everybody likes cod. Separating those great, juicy flakes and bathing them in a well-made parsley sauce and a scoop of creamy mashed potato may be nursery food, but it is the sort of nursery to have a great deal of prelapsarian charm.

The mussel soup is classic, too, but from a posher tradition of fine French restaurants. It can be prepared a day in advance (up to liquidising and sieving it), as can the lemon tart, which is even better the next day. I learnt how to make this when I worked at Le Gavroche and have changed the recipe only slightly over the years. Most of what I know I learnt from the great Albert Roux during my time there and this recipe represents as well as anything his style of cooking – sumptuous but clean and unfussed in its interpretation of flavour. It is not easy to make but you owe it to yourself to try: after a couple of attempts you will have perfected one of the truly great desserts.

MUSSEL SOUP

2kg mussels
¼ bottle of dry white wine
2 onions
2 carrots
4 cloves of garlic
1 leek
50g unsalted butter
3 overripe tomatoes
A handful of rice
A pinch of saffron
A sprig of thyme
1 teaspoon cracked pepper
150ml double cream

Thin slices of baguette, fried in olive oil and rubbed with garlic, are a very welcome addition to this soup.

Wash the mussels, discarding any open ones that refuse to close when tapped on a work surface. Put them in a big pan with a glass of the white wine, cover and briefly steam them open, shaking the pan occasionally. The minute the mussels open, drain them in a big colander, taking care to catch all the liquid in a voluminous bowl underneath.

Peel the onions, carrots and garlic and slice them finely, together with the well-washed leek.

Melt the butter in the pan and stew these vegetables gently while you pick the mussels from their shells. Strain the cooking liquid through a very fine sieve, taking care not to let any of the grit at the bottom of the bowl through.

Chop the tomatoes roughly and add to the pan when the other vegetables have softened. Add half the mussels, the rest of the white wine, the mussel juice, rice, saffron, thyme and pepper.

Bring gently to the boil and then add 500ml of water (or fish stock, if you happen to have it) and simmer gently for half an hour.

When the soup is cooked, liquidise it in a blender to make a really smooth purée and then pass it through a sieve, pushing it through with the back of a spoon or ladle (a deep conical sieve is an asset in this sort of operation).

Gently reheat the soup with the double cream and the remaining mussels, check the seasoning and then serve.

Variation: with carrots and dill

Omit half the rice, the saffron and the cream from the preceding recipe and add:

200g carrots
50g butter
Sugar
½ bunch of dill

Make the soup in exactly the same way. Peel the carrots and slice them very finely. Put them in a pan with the butter, a pinch each of sugar and salt, and enough water to cover. Place a buttered paper over them and cook on a medium heat until the carrots are tender and the water has evaporated.

Chop the dill, not too finely, and add. Add the mussels that have not been liquidised in the soup and pour the strained soup over this garnish.

COD WITH PARSLEY SAUCE

6 fillets or steaks of cod, weighing
*   200–230g each*
Plain flour
2 tablespoons sunflower oil
25g unsalted butter

For the parsley sauce:

25g unsalted butter
25g plain flour
500ml milk
The head or bones of the fish
1 large onion, peeled and sliced
6 cloves
A sprig of thyme
2 bay leaves
A pinch of nutmeg
A good bunch of parsley, flat-leaf or
*   curly*
100ml single cream

The old way of making this sauce, by poaching the cod in milk and thickening the liquor thus produced, kept the fish hanging around too long after it was cooked, making it tired and flaccid. Much better to make the sauce first and serve up a zingy piece of fresh fish, just cooked and still moist in the middle. If you don't want to fry or 'roast' the fish, steam rather than poach it, as the flesh of a cod is surprisingly delicate and falls apart very easily.

For the sauce, melt the butter in a saucepan and add the flour. Stir for a minute or two to make a sandy roux, then add the milk, a few tablespoons at a time initially, until a smooth paste is formed. Add the rest of the milk and whisk together as the mixture comes slowly to the boil.

Now add the fish head or bones, the sliced onion, cloves, thyme, bay leaves and nutmeg. Season with sea salt and milled white pepper and simmer extremely gently on the side of the stove. Dilute with a little more milk if the sauce gets too thick and continue to cook for twenty-five minutes.

Pick the parsley from its stalks and rinse it well, then shake it dry and chop finely with a large knife. Strain the sauce through a fine sieve into a fresh saucepan and add the parsley and cream. Bring to the boil and taste for seasoning. Simmer to reduce a little if the sauce is too thin.

Season the cod very well with sea salt and white pepper before dredging it in flour. Heat the oil and butter in a large frying pan and, when foaming, shake off any excess flour from the fish and put it in the pan – skin-side down if using fillets.

Moderate the heat slightly and cook the fish for four to seven minutes, depending on thickness. To prevent the pieces sticking, shake the pan occasionally and keep the fish moving. Turn the fish and cook the other side, removing it when you can feel the flakes separating under the surface.

Serve immediately, surrounded by plenty of sauce and an equally good quantity of creamy mashed potatoes (see page 38).

LEMON TART

2 lemons
4 eggs plus 1 yolk
150g caster sugar
150ml double cream
Icing sugar for dusting

For the pastry:

120g unsalted butter
180g plain flour
50g caster sugar
2 egg yolks
1 egg
1 tablespoon milk

I am afraid a high-sided tart ring or tin, 22cm wide and 3cm high, is essential here, unless you have two low-sided rings that you can put on top of each other. It is absolutely vital that the case is leakproof; after that, it is almost a doddle.

First make the pastry. Cut the butter into very small dice without letting it warm up too much. Put the flour, sugar, butter and a pinch of salt in a large bowl and rub them together using only your fingertips.

Alternatively this can be done with the blending attachment of an electric mixer on the slowest speed. The mixture should be completely blended to a sandy texture with no lumps of butter remaining. Make a well in the centre, then whisk the egg yolks with two tablespoons of cold water and pour them into the well. Very gently blend the mixture together to form a dough. Shape into a slightly flattened ball, wrap in clingfilm and refrigerate for one hour.

Butter and flour the inside of the tart ring. Roll out the pastry on a lightly floured surface to a disc at least 30cm in diameter – this allows for the depth of the ring and for overlapping the sides by a minimum of a centimetre. Carefully drop the pastry into the ring, making sure it fits right into the corners and hangs over the edge at every point. Do not cut off this overhang. Make absolutely sure there are no holes in the pastry, using any excess overhang to carry out repairs. Refrigerate the case for thirty minutes.

Line the pastry case with greaseproof paper or foil and fill with baking beans. Bake for twenty minutes in an oven preheated to 180°C / Gas Mark 4.

Remove the beans and paper and return the case to the oven for five minutes to finish cooking. Beat the egg and milk together and brush over the interior of the case the minute it comes out of the oven and is still very hot.

For the filling, finely grate the lemon zest into a bowl and then strain the well-squeezed juice over. Whisk the eggs and sugar together until the sugar is dissolved and the mixture is smooth. Pour in the double cream. Mix together well and then stir in the lemon juice and zest.

Lower the oven temperature to 120°C / Gas Mark ½. Place the tart ring on the middle shelf of the oven, a third of the way out of the oven. Carefully pour in the mixture (stir it well beforehand if you have let it rest) and slide the tart very carefully into the oven. It will take an hour and three-quarters to cook. The surface should not colour: if it threatens to do so, be prepared to cover it with a sheet of foil. To test, give the tray a gentle nudge back and forth – there should be no sign of liquid movement beneath the surface of the tart.

Allow the tart to cool a little before sawing off the pastry overhang with a serrated knife and gently lifting off the tart ring.

Transfer the tart to a plate only when it has completely cooled, then refrigerate. Dust with a sprinkling of icing sugar and serve chilled.

PART OF THE PHENOMENON...

of our decreasing vocabulary of food is the fault of lawyers. The growth of the personal injury business has served my siblings well (both my brother and sister are in the racket, albeit on different sides), but, in my view, it transfers the blame to the wrong quarter.

Take fish bones: is the act of choking on a fish bone the fault of the careless eater or the provider? If it is the latter, he or she has no option but to abandon the notion of serving fish on the bone. There is a similar problem with game: if, as a chef, I serve a game bird and a customer breaks an expensive piece of dentistry on a piece of shot, am I seriously to blame? Is there no caveat emptor, does not everyone realise that game must be shot, and that it is impossible to remove, or guarantee to remove, every piece of lead in the carcass? Again, we will all ultimately lose out if it becomes impossible to serve game.

The whole situation would appear to be a law of diminishing returns. In the wake of the great salmonella crisis, logic would suggest that serious efforts would be made to eradicate the disease from the nation's flock. No such luck: instead, the use of eggs has become a high-risk activity for hotels and restaurants. No self-respecting caterer will now make mayonnaise with fresh eggs, or run the risk of serving undercooked eggs.

It is a classic case of killing the messenger and letting the message go by unread. At least when cooking at home we are still immune from these worries.

BOXING DAY LUNCH

SHRIMP PASTE

BRAISED HAM WITH CUMBERLAND SAUCE AND MACARONI GRATIN

PAVLOVA WITH KIWI AND PASSION FRUIT

Serves 8

Ham is not posh. Parma ham certainly is, and individual English cured hams, such as York and Bradenham, likewise have a certain cachet, but ham, or green gammon, is decidedly, well, common. Ham is so downright common partly because it is the most available and inexpensive meat acceptable to children. Although most consider pigs rather disgusting and would not dream of eating one, they find thin, pink slices of watery ham perfectly all right. Somehow, the action of the salt is the completion of a transformation from pig via pork to ham that renders the meat innocuous and untainted.

Ham used to be common for rather different reasons. Peasants kept pigs, like geese, because they were economical to raise, needed little land and ate pretty much everything. They ceased to be economical to keep in winter, so they were slaughtered in the autumn and salted down for the cold months when fresh meat was less available. The whole repertoire of charcuterie, whether in France, Italy or Britain, whether it be rillettes, a salame or a Dunmow flitch, is based on this simple exigency.

Perhaps because of its farmyard familiarity, not even the ham, the grandest piece of the pig, has ever featured at the top tables. You are still more likely to find a decent fresh cooked ham in a country pub than in a swanky restaurant in town. Despite Napoleon in *Animal Farm*, the pig is a democratic creature and ham the food of the people.

Boxing Day, when Christmas boxes were traditionally given out, is equally democratic in spirit, and the perfect time to cook a whole gammon. There is always enough to go round, and there is no hierarchy of white meat and red meat to worry the carver. The cook does not have a lot to worry about either. Given enough time, a ham is deliriously easy to cook. It needs a day's soaking, a preliminary blanching, two to three hours' simmering and a final hour's roasting. If you do not have a ham kettle or a pot big enough, there is no cause for alarm as the ham can be entirely baked in the oven instead of boiling it first. Half fill a deep oven tray with water, place the ham on a trivet or rack suspended above the tray, cover it with foil and bake in a slow oven for five to six hours before finishing, dry, in a much hotter oven. Either way should produce a beautifully moist ham with a crisp and shiny glaze that is downright festive.

I always serve Cumberland sauce, usually in a semi-set sort of condition, with my ham. It can be made well in advance and is always a revelation to those who have not had a proper one before. Then I tend to go mad on vegetables, usually offering four or five with different textures and degrees of complication. Cabbage cakes, macaroni gratin, Brussels sprouts might turn up. But if you are not up to it, there are always frozen peas. The ham, of course, will do fifteen people quite happily but half the point is to have some really good ham kicking around in the fridge afterwards. The rest of the menu will serve eight comfortably.

SHRIMP PASTE

1kg cooked shrimps
500g whiting fillet, or other soft, flaky fish
Powdered mace
Cayenne pepper
450g butter, softened, plus some melted butter

There is a touching description of a Yorkshire shrimp tea in Dorothy Hartley's book, *Food in England*, but we are talking lunch, and brown bread and butter, or Melba toast. This is what she calls 'Betty Tatterstall's best', and very good it is too.

Shell the shrimps, reserve the tails and put the shells and heads in a pan with enough cold water to cover. Boil for twenty minutes and then strain. Cook the fish in this liquor until it flakes easily and then strain, keeping the liquor. Pound the fish to a smooth paste (in a food processor, if you have it) with a judicious seasoning of powdered mace and cayenne. Add as much cooking liquor back into the paste as you can without letting it become mushy, then add the softened butter and mix until completely smooth. Fold in the shrimps (not in the food processor) and decant into fine white china. Smooth the surface and finish with a little melted butter to make a seal.

BRAISED HAM

1 ham, weighing 8–10kg
Cloves
3 onions
4 carrots
1 head of celery
A few sprigs of parsley and thyme
2 bay leaves
Peppercorns
3 tablespoons brown sugar
300ml white wine
1 teaspoon potato flour or cornflour

I prefer to bone the ham – it certainly facilitates carving – and your butcher should be happy to do all the hard work for you, given a bit of warning. Ask him to score the skin in diagonal lines, criss-cross fashion, while he's at it, and then tie it.

A huge braising pan will do for both cooking processes: otherwise it's a big pot to cook it in and a roasting dish for the final braise.

Soak the ham in a bucket of cold water for twenty-four hours. Put it in a pot of cold water on the stove and bring to the boil.

Drain this water and stud the ham with cloves at the interstices of the scoring. Cover again with cold water and bring to the boil.

Halve one of the onions and peel two of the carrots. Add to the pot together with three outside ribs of the celery. Make a bouquet garni with the herbs and add this to the pot, along with a small handful of peppercorns.

Poach the ham in this stock on a very gentle heat for two and a half hours.

Lift the ham out of the stock (two strong roasting forks are the best weapons) and place on a chopping board. Strain the stock. Remove the string from the ham and peel off the skin, taking care to leave as much fat behind as possible. Put the ham in a roasting tin and place in an oven preheated to 230°C / Gas Mark 8.

Chop up the remaining vegetables. After ten minutes, sprinkle the sugar over the ham and arrange the chopped vegetables around it. Let the ham caramelise for another twenty minutes.

The vegetables should be well browned in the rendered fat and juices. Pour in all but half a glassful of the white wine, cover the ham with a lid or foil and braise for thirty minutes. Test with a skewer to check the ham is cooked: it must be hot all the way through. Lift on to a serving dish and keep warm.

Mix the potato flour or cornflour with the remaining wine and whisk it into the gravy. Add 200ml of the ham stock and simmer for ten minutes, until reduced. Check the seasoning and strain.

Take the beautifully glazed ham to the table and carve thin slices down towards the bone, twisting the knife at the very end in order to detach the slice from the joint. Serve with the gravy.

Let everyone help themselves to the multitude of accompaniments, not forgetting some good mustard.

CUMBERLAND SAUCE

450g redcurrant jelly
3 oranges
1 lemon
3 shallots
A good piece of fresh root ginger
Butter
1 tablespoon mustard powder
350ml port (grocer's, nothing fancy)

It's worth making plenty of this, since it goes with all manner of meats, but especially ham, hot or cold. It keeps very well.

Put the redcurrant jelly in a bowl placed over a pan of simmering water to melt. With a fine peeler, remove the zest of the oranges and lemon, leaving the bitter white pith behind. Halve the fruit and squeeze the juice. Slice the zest into very fine julienne, put it in a little saucepan with some cold water and bring to the boil. Simmer for three minutes and then drain the julienne and cool in some cold water.

Peel the shallots and ginger, cut them into very fine julienne and stew very gently in a small knob of butter for ten minutes. Add the blanched orange and lemon zest, the juice and the mustard powder. Let these simmer until the liquid is reduced to a syrup. Add plenty of milled pepper and the port and simmer until reduced by half. Add the melted redcurrant jelly, whisk well, then remove from the heat and leave to cool.

MACARONI GRATIN

1 onion
6 cloves
2 bay leaves
A large sprig of thyme
2 parsley stalks
750ml milk
50g butter
50g plain flour
500g long macaroni
4 egg yolks
250ml double cream
125g Gruyère, grated
75g Parmesan, grated

Not just any macaroni cheese, this: to start with, you need proper, thick, long macaroni, not those silly little plumbing tubes usually on offer. And not just any cheese, I'm afraid. Decent Gruyère in the sauce and fresh grated Parmesan on top make a huge difference.

Peel the onion and stud it with the cloves. Make a bouquet garni with the herbs. Cover both in the milk, bring to the boil, then remove from the heat and leave to infuse for one hour.

Melt the butter in a saucepan and stir in the flour to make a roux. Cook for a couple of minutes, stirring constantly, and then work in a couple of tablespoons of the milk with a wooden spoon to make a smooth paste. Add the rest of the milk and whisk well to ensure a smooth sauce as it comes back to the boil.

Using a heat diffuser or simmering mat, cook out the sauce on the gentlest of heats for fifteen minutes.

Bring a big pot of salted water to the boil and simmer the macaroni in it for ten to twelve minutes, until just cooked. Meanwhile, whisk together the egg yolks and cream and pour the hot sauce over them, whisking well. Return to the heat for a couple of minutes. Add plenty of milled pepper and the Gruyère and remove from the heat, stirring well to melt the cheese. Season if necessary.

Drain the macaroni when cooked and then mix immediately with the sauce. Pour into a large shallow dish, sprinkle with the grated Parmesan and finish in a hot oven for fifteen minutes or until bubbling hot and golden brown on top.

PAVLOVA WITH KIWI AND PASSION FRUIT

1 orange
1 teaspoon cornflour
500g caster sugar, plus 1 tablespoon
9 egg whites
1 teaspoon vinegar
8 passion fruit
350ml double cream
6 kiwi fruit

Part of the charm of the pavlova is the artless way in which the meringue is spooned on to the tray. It is the alleged resemblance to a ballerina's tutu that may have given it its name. Look for well-wizened, crinkled passion fruit, as they have the most juice.

Finely grate the zest of half the orange. Sift together the cornflour and sugar and add the orange zest. Beat the egg whites with an electric whisk until they form stiff peaks, then add the vinegar. Beat in a third of the sugar and cornflour, then gently fold in the remainder with a large kitchen spoon. Spoon the mixture on to a baking tray lined with baking parchment and form a circle about 27cm in diameter. Make a small well in the centre of the meringue and shape the edges into swirly hillocks with the back of the spoon. Place the pavlova in an oven preheated to 150°C / Gas Mark 2 for thirty minutes, or until it takes on a mere hint of colour. Turn the oven down to 130°C / Gas Mark 1–2 and leave the pavlova to cook for fifty minutes. Do not open the oven door after this time but switch the oven off and leave the pavlova in it for a further two hours. It should be miraculously light but still have a sticky interior.

Cut the passion fruit in half and scoop out the seeds into a bowl. Dilute with a tablespoon of juice from the orange and then break up the seeds with a fork. Whip the cream with the tablespoon of caster sugar until it forms soft peaks and then fold in the passion fruit and orange juice mixture. Continue beating until quite stiff. Spoon this mixture into the well of the pavlova. Peel the kiwi fruit, slice them into rounds and stick into the cream mixture in a random fashion.

IT IS ALWAYS A REFRESHING SPECTACLE TO SEE...

Australia lose a match. It is a shame that the match in question is not cricket, nor is it against us, but a more localised dispute with their distant neighbours in New Zealand.

The Pavlova War has been rumbling on for some years. Since neither side has been able to boast much in the way of a contribution to global gastronomy until recently, both are anxious to claim this classic dish for their own. Both sides, too, are keen to distinguish a pavlova from an ordinary meringue: in the addition of vinegar and cornflour to the egg whites, there hangs a thread with which a national cuisine is woven.

The Australian claim dates from 1934, when the chef of the Esplanade Hotel in Perth, one Bert Sachse, was summoned by the owner, Mrs Elizabeth Paxton, and told to produce "something special". Answering the command, he told a reporter afterwards that he had "always regretted that the meringue cake was invariably too hard and crusty", so he "set out to create something that could have a crunchy top and would cut like marshmallow". After the crucial development with the cornflour and vinegar, the new cake, filled with cream and festooned with passion fruit, was presented to a delighted Mrs Paxton, who swooned and declared the new addition to the repertoire to be "as light as Pavlova".

A variation on the Australian myth declares the dish to have been named in honour of the Russian ballerina who was touring Australia at the time. Even the great Jane Grigson is duped by the Aussie myth and asserts that Pavlova visited the subcontinent "in the Thirties". There is a slight problem with this presentation of history, since the first Australian reference to pavlova, the cake, postdates the premature death in 1931 of Pavlova, the great dancer, by some three years. If these anomalies are not enough to raise one's suspicions, there are several references to a pavlova cake in New Zealand that predate Bert Sachse's epiphany in a Perth hotel in 1934. Davis Gelatine (NZ) Ltd published a recipe for pavlova in 1927, in a nifty volume published in Auckland and entitled *Davis' Dainty Dishes*, which would seem to pull the middle stump of the Australian wicket right out of the ground.

The New Zealanders are not entirely disingenuous themselves. They have demonstrated a canny sense of presentation in these matters. When they had no luck with their initial efforts to sell Chinese goose-berries in the United States, they appropriated the fruit in the Sixties and rechristened it the kiwi.

The rest is nouvelle cuisine, and history. A few years later, they performed the same trick with the strange tree tomato and came up with the more likely-sounding tamarillo.

THE VEGETARIAN IN LENT

CRÈME PALESTINE

CABBAGE CAKE WITH MOZZARELLA AND DRIED CEPS

BISCOTTI AND VIN SANTO ICE CREAM

Serves 6

Food is not the be all and end all of life – there is something distasteful in being too well fed – and there are times when it is wise to lay off for a bit. Traditionally, of course, this was a communal act, since everybody abstained, or was supposed to, during Lent.

This was not just a piece of post-Saturnalia belt-tightening but also a result of necessity. There simply was not that much food about. For all the plenitude of the winter storecupboard, things began to look a little grim by March. The frosts put paid to most crops and game, while the salted meat was getting both monotonous and progressively less abundant.

It takes a period of abstinence to appreciate properly what there is. This is the crux of the argument for seasonality in food. If asparagus or strawberries taste better for being unavailable eleven months of the year, so, too, does good food taste better after a lay-off.

I know that in this book I have gone over the top from time to time. All chefs do it. Some of these menus are a lot of food. Often I have recommended a three-course meal when even two might seem a lot. Munch on a few olives instead of a starter. Instead of pudding, offer fruit. Omit the main course, even, and have some bread and cheese or a plate of pasta. Chefs, however, are not nutritionists, and going without does not make a cookbook.

Just because there is a time for asceticism does not mean we should not care what we eat. There is never anything wrong with a proper concern for good food. Here is a worthy Lenten menu, to be served in the best-behaved company, with a little Vin Santo to bless the proceedings.

CRÈME PALESTINE

1 white onion
400g Jerusalem artichokes
Butter
200g potatoes
600ml milk
500ml water
A sprig of thyme
1 bay leaf
100g hazelnuts
100ml double cream
Hazelnut oil and very finely chopped
   chives, to serve (optional)

Peel and slice the onion and Jerusalem artichokes. Stew the onion in a little butter for a few minutes, then add the artichokes and stew gently for twenty minutes. Peel and chop the potatoes and add to the pan with the milk, water, herbs and some salt and pepper. Bring to the boil and then cook for thirty minutes on a gentle heat. Meanwhile, toast the hazelnuts, rub them in a dry cloth to remove the skins and chop them coarsely.

Purée the soup in a blender or pass it through the finest disc on a mouli, taking care to remove the bay leaf first. Return to the pan and bring back to the boil, then whisk in the cream and pour into a warmed tureen. Now sprinkle the chopped hazelnuts on to the hot soup.

A little hazelnut oil can be trickled over at this point and the whole sprinkled with very finely chopped chives. There's no crime in dispensing with all this embellishment altogether, of course: the soup will do very well, plain and simple.

CABBAGE CAKE WITH MOZZARELLA AND DRIED CEPS

40g dried ceps
2 cloves of garlic
2 dessertspoons virgin olive oil
1 large Savoy cabbage
Butter
250g mozzarella
400g tinned plum tomatoes
1 teaspoon sugar
A sprig of thyme

I usually make this dish with a few chopped salted anchovies instead of the ceps, but this variation will find more favour with genuine vegetarians.

Soak the ceps in cold water for one hour, then drain and chop very finely. Chop one of the garlic cloves extremely finely and stew it very gently in a dessertspoonful of the olive oil before adding the ceps. Stew this ensemble on the lowest possible heat for ten minutes.

Remove the outer leaves of the cabbage and wash them well in plenty of cold water.

Drop into a large pan of boiling salted water and simmer for about two minutes, then remove and refresh in plenty of cold water to fix the colour. Cut out the central stalks and dry the leaves very well on kitchen paper. Cut the cabbage heart into quarters, then bring the water back to the boil and drop them in. Simmer until tender and then drain. Refresh the cabbage heart in cold water and squeeze dry very thoroughly.

Take a flat-bottomed, earthenware dish and butter it well. Put the most handsome leaf in the bottom. It should practically fill it. Overlapping them bountifully, line the sides of the dish with the rest of the leaves so that they overhang and will make a cover. Cut away the stalk from the cabbage heart. Separate the leaves and layer a third of them in the dish with plenty of pepper and a little sea salt. Dot with butter or olive oil, or both. Thinly slice the mozzarella, lay half of it on top of the cabbage and then add half the cep mixture, sprinkling it over the surface. Repeat with more cabbage, mozzarella and ceps and close the outside leaves over the whole assembly. Dot with more butter and bake in an oven preheated to 220°C / Gas Mark 7 for twenty minutes, or until the cheese melts and the outside starts to brown. Meanwhile, make a

tomato sauce: chop the second clove of garlic finely and stew for a moment in the remaining dessertspoon of olive oil. Coarsely chop the tinned tomatoes, add them to the pan with the sugar, thyme and a good seasoning of salt and pepper, then simmer until reduced and thickened. Liquidise the sauce and pass through a sieve before reheating gently.

Turn the cabbage cake out on to a plate and serve with the tomato sauce.

BISCOTTI

500g plain flour
4 eggs, beaten
500g caster sugar
½ teaspoon baking powder
200g blanched almonds
150g pine nuts
2 teaspoons fennel seeds
1 teaspoon grated lemon zest

This recipe makes some fifty biscotti, which may seem rather a lot. Put them in an airtight tin and, once you get in the habit of nibbling them with coffee, they will not hang around for long.

Sift the flour on to a board, make a well in the centre and pour in the beaten eggs. Gather in the flour and mix well. Add the sugar, baking powder and a pinch of salt and mix well. Chop the almonds very coarsely and add to the mixture, along with the pine nuts, fennel seeds and lemon zest. Knead well to make a firm dough, making sure the nuts are well distributed. Shape the dough into two rolls about 4cm in diameter. Place these rolls on a greased baking tray and bake in an oven preheated to 200°C / Gas Mark 6 for fifteen minutes. The dough must still be soft in the middle.

Let the rolls cool a little and then put them on a board. With a sharp serrated knife, cut them, on a slight diagonal if necessary, into biscuits 10cm long and about 8mm thick. Put the biscuits back on the baking tray and return to the oven for ten minutes. Turn them over and cook for ten minutes more. Cool on a wire rack and then store in an airtight container.

BISCOTTI AND VIN SANTO ICE CREAM

8 egg yolks
100g caster sugar
500ml milk
150g biscotti
100ml Vin Santo
225ml whipping cream

A good use for leftover biscotti, or if you have an excess of crumbs. A good sweet sherry is a perfectly acceptable substitute if you have drunk all the Vin Santo. I am afraid an ice-cream machine is essential.

Whisk the egg yolks and sugar together really well until the mixture whitens and increases in volume. Bring the milk to the boil and slowly pour a quarter of it into the egg yolk and sugar mixture, whisking constantly. Pour this mixture back into the milk and return to a gentle heat. With a wooden spoon, stir the mixture constantly, taking care to reach all the corners and the base of the pan. Like any custard, it will thicken almost imperceptibly. Check the consistency by running your finger over the back of the spoon: it is thick enough when the spoon is coated and the trail of your finger is clearly visible. Remove immediately from the heat and pour into a bowl (strain it if you are nervous about the possibility of lumps). Leave to cool.

Chop the biscotti coarsely, pour over the Vin Santo and leave to macerate for five minutes. Whip the cream to the 'ribbon', i.e. when the cream on the end of a whisk leaves a trail on the cream in the bowl. Take care not to overwhip. When the custard mixture has chilled, pour it into the whipped cream, stirring well. Fold in the biscotti and Vin Santo mixture, pour into the ice-cream machine and churn.

NOTHING COULD BE MORE TYPICALLY FAR-FETCHED...

in the world of *haute cuisine* than the name 'Crème Palestine'. The Jerusalem artichoke is a tall, gangling plant with large flowers that turn, like sunflowers, with the sun. This confusion with the sunflower led to them being dubbed girasole and, just as Cockney traders shorten and transmute 'asparagus' to 'grass', 'girasole' became 'Jerusalem'. Escoffier, or another hotel chef working in England, dubbed the soup 'Palestine' on account of this spurious association, since it was the fashion then to obfuscate and mystify dishes by giving them names.

These days we seek to describe a dish when we name it on a menu and would, if using French, give it the simple but sonorous title of 'Crème des Topinambours'. Even the French get confused here. My head chef at Le Gavroche consistently referred to parsnips as *topinambours*, although that root has the perfectly good, if more prosaic-sounding, French name of *panais*.

The French, generally, will not eat their topinambours. For some reason there were no potatoes to be had during the war and people turned to the Jerusalem artichoke. It is a delicious vegetable, but no substitute for the potato. They grew to hate this vegetable they felt had been thrust upon them, just as the British grew to hate rabbit. That particular hatred evinced itself in the notorious myxomatosis campaign in the early Fifties, a deliberate attempt to exterminate the whole rabbit population from which it took some thirty years to recover.

That little confusion explained, there is still no clue as to why those misshapen tubers should be confused with the thistle-like globe artichoke, since they have no botanical or gastronomic similarity. It is a long road to Jerusalem.

GLOSSARY

Ceps Found in the wild in late September, October and November. There are many other forms of *Boletus* for which they can be mistaken and which make reasonable eating but the deep, savoury flavour of the *Boletus edulis* puts it in a class of its own.

Escarole This mild member of the chicory family has large, thick, white leaves, pale green at the edges.

Grouse Perhaps the finest of game birds, grouse are at their best in September.

John Dory This flat fish is easily recognised by its telescopic mouth and the mark of St Peter, a black spot just behind the head. It has firm, white fillets of densely textured meat. Similar to brill and turbot, small ones are much cheaper than large but just as delicious.

Mirabelles These tiny yellow plums are grown in France and picked in the last three weeks of August. When fully ripe, they blush a lovely crimson through their yellow skins before they finally burst with sugar.

Morels are the spring rival to ceps as the finest wild mushroom. They have a succulent texture and deep flavour, and their deeply ridged or corrugated caps absorb buttery and creamy sauces beautifully. They also dry extremely well.

Mozzarella Proper Mozzarella is made with buffalo milk in southern Italy, mostly just south of Naples. Although low in fat, it is rich in flavour. It is highly perishable and should be eaten very fresh.

Oysters are basically divided into two types: natives, which are round, and rocks, which are long and thin. Although natives are superior raw, they are at least twice the price and I always cook with rocks.

Partridge Like oysters, partridges fall into two types. The native, wild English greyleg has a much stronger, gamier flavour and is superb *à l'anglaise*, that is to say, simply roasted and served with a gravy, bread sauce and game chips. To make Chartreuse, the slightly plumper, more tender French redleg partridge is more appropriate.

Pheasant Plentiful in December and January when other game birds have finished, hen birds are smaller, have less fat and are more tender than cocks.

Pimenton This is Spanish paprika and has an earthy, smoky flavour that dominates much Spanish cooking and can be found in delightful little red tins.

Polenta is ground maize, picked and dried in the autumn.

Quinces Shaped like large, fat pears with a yellow skin covered in soft down, quinces have tough, inedible flesh when raw. Cooked, they turn a beautiful dark pink colour, give off a rich, musky scent and have a deep and subtle flavour.

Red Mullet Although plentiful in winter, they are more associated with summer food. When really fresh, they have long, golden lines running the length of the fish.

Rhubarb is perfectly common in late spring and early summer. The very best is the delicate, early forced champagne rhubarb produced from January to March.

Salsify is a long, tapering brown root. It is often confused with scorzonera, which is easier to work with and there is no discernible difference in flavour.

Scallops Best sold in the shell when still alive. If this is not possible check they have not been soaked in water to increase their weight. Soaked scallops will be puffed up and white, whereas fresh unsoaked scallops will be a pearly opalescent colour and very firm.

Sea Kale Our only indigenous vegetable, sea kale is now extremely hard to find.

Sea Trout are in season from March to June. Difficult to find, it would be better to substitute a good salmon rather than the ubiquitous farmed trout.

Skirt Steak This is the name given to two different internal muscles, found frequently in Parisian brasseries as *onglet* or *bavette*. They both become tough when overcooked but have a superb flavour.

Tamarillos are an exotic fruit sometimes known as tree tomatoes but are not the same as tomatillos.

Veal is still mostly imported from Holland, where it is reared in circumstances many feel is inhumane though some good English veal is available, some of it under the Freedom Food imprimature.

Venison is extremely plentiful in Britain. The three main types are the tiny roe deer, with very fine, dark meat; the fallow, slightly larger, the meat paler and less strong; and the plentiful red, with strong, dark meat.

Wild Strawberries These are not usually wild but cultivated Alpine varieties.

INDEX

Almonds
Chilled avocado and almond soup 60
Greengage and almond tart 74
Anchovies
Bagna cauda sauce 50
Penne with broccoli, garlic and anchovies 118
Piedmontese peppers 66
Purple sprouting broccoli with anchovies and olive oil 16
Salade Niçoise 54, 57
Apples 115
Tarte Tatin 108, 110
Asparagus
Asparagus and morels 25
Risotto primavera 78
Aubergines
Bruschetta with grilled aubergines and roast garlic paste 48
Imam Bayildi 113
Red mullet, aubergine and potato sandwich 61
Tian of tomatoes and aubergines 68
Avocados
Chilled avocado and almond soup 60

Basil: Grilled tomatoes and fennel with basil 50
Beans
boiling 135
Le Cassoulet 133
Risotto primavera 78
Salade Niçoise 54, 57
Beef
cooking a steak 31
Skirt steak with shallots 30
Biscotti 252
Biscotti and Vin Santo ice cream 153
Blackcurrants: Summer pudding 69
Bread
Bread sauce 89
Bruschetta with grilled aubergines and roast garlic paste 48
Cream of fennel soup with tapenade croutons 112
Summer pudding 69

Broccoli
Penne with broccoli, garlic and anchovies 118
Purple sprouting broccoli with anchovies and olive oil 16
Cabbage
Cabbage cake with mozzarella and dried ceps 151
Chartreuse of partridge 106
Celeriac mash 40
Ceps
Cabbage cake with mozzarella and dried ceps 151
Potato and cep cake 94
Champ 39
Cheese 115
Aligot 40
Cabbage cake with mozzarella and dried ceps 151
Courgette and gorgonzola risotto 78
Escarole, pear and Roquefort salad 98
Greek salad 73
Pumpkin soup with cream and Gruyère 105
Chestnuts: Venison stew with baby onions, chestnuts and chocolate 99
Chicken
Cream of chicken and mushroom soup 13
Roast chicken with tarragon 67
Chilli
Grilled pineapple with chilli syrup and coconut ice cream 102
Spaghetti with crab, garlic, and chilli 118
Chocolate
Chocolate tart with crème fraiche 26
Rich chocolate mousse 16
Venison stew with baby onions, chestnuts and chocolate 99
Cinnamon
Baked quinces with cinnamon and Vin Santo 129
Cinnamon ice cream 95
Coconut
Grilled pineapple with chilli syrup and coconut ice cream 102
Cod with parsley sauce 139
Coffee bean sauce 17
Coriander: Lamb kebabs with coriander and cumin 49
Courgettes and gorgonzola risotto 78

INDEX

Crab
Crab and papaya salad 29
Spaghetti with crab, garlic, and chilli 118
Cream
Braised pheasant with cream and pimenton 127
Crème Palestine 151
Pumpkin soup with cream and Gruyère 105
Crème fraiche: Chocolate tart with crème fraiche 26
Cumin: Lamb kebabs with coriander and cumin 49
Custard: Mirabelles and custard 90

Duck 63
Le Cassoulet 133
Roast duck with peas 35

Eggs
Pavlova with kiwi and passion fruit 147
Rich chocolate mousse 16
Salade Niçoise 54, 57
Escarole, pear and Roquefort salad 98

Fennel
Cream of fennel soup with tapenade croutons 112
Grilled tomatoes and fennel with basil 50
Potato, fennel and rosemary risotto 79
Figs
Parma ham with figs 93
Fish, frying 64

Garlic
Breast of veal with pork, spinach and garlic stuffing 55
Bruschetta with grilled aubergines and roast garlic paste 48
Penne with broccoli, garlic and anchovies 118
Quick roast potatoes with onions, garlic and rosemary 41
Roast garlic mash 40
Roast loin of pork with herbs and garlic 73
Spaghetti with crab, garlic, and chilli 118
Ginger: Raw salmon with ginger dressing 34
Greengage and almond tart 74
Grouse: Roast grouse 89

Ham
Braised ham 145
Parma ham with figs 93
Haricot beans
Le Cassoulet 133

Hollandaise: Sea kale with blood orange hollandaise 21
Horseradish: Sea trout fillet with a horseradish crust 21

Ice cream
Baked tamarillos with vanilla ice cream 31
Cinnamon ice cream 95
Grilled pineapple with chilli syrup and coconut ice cream 102

Jerusalem artichokes
Crème Palestine 151
Jerusalem artichoke mash 40
John Dory with rhubarb 25

Kiwi: Pavlova with kiwi and passion fruit 147

Lamb 29
Lamb kebabs with coriander and cumin 49
Le Cassoulet 133
Roast leg of lamb with persillade 14

Lemon
Escarole, pear and Roquefort salad 98
Lemon tart 140
Red onions with sage and lemon 49
Tarte Tatin 108, 110

Macaroni gratin 146
Marinade 51
Shish kebab marinade 51
Milk: New potatoes in milk 40
Mint: Griddled scallops with pea purée and mint vinaigrette 126, 130
Mirabelles 138
bottling 91
Mirabelles and custard 90
Morels: Asparagus and morels 25
Mozzarella: Cabbage cake with mozzarella and dried ceps 151
Mushrooms
Asparagus and morels 25
Cream of chicken and mushroom soup 13
Potato and cep cake 94
Wild mushroom risotto 93
Mussels
Fettuccine with mussels 116
Mussel soup 138

Olive oil
Purple sprouting broccoli with anchovies and olive oil 16
Saffron and olive oil mash 39
Sauternes and olive oil cake with red fruit salad 56
Onions
Greek salad 73
Oyster and onion tart 87
Quick roast potatoes with onions, garlic and rosemary 41
Red onions with sage and lemon 49
Shish kebab marinade 51
Venison stew with baby onions, chestnuts and chocolate 99
Oranges
Sea kale with blood orange hollandaise 21
Oyster and onion tart 87

Papaya: Crab and papaya salad 29
Parsley
Cod with parsley sauce 139
Parsley mash 39
Parsnip mash 40
Partridge: Chartreuse of partridge 106
Passion fruit: Pavlova with kiwi and passion fruit 147
Pasta 115, 116
Fettuccine with mussels 116
Macaroni gratin 146
Penne with broccoli, garlic and anchovies 118
Spaghetti with crab, garlic, and chilli 118
Tagliatelle al ragu 117
Pears
Escarole, pear and Roquefort salad 98
Poached pears in Beaujolais 95
Peas
Griddled scallops with pea purée and mint vinaigrette 126, 130
Risotto primavera 78
Roast duck with peas 35
Peppers: Piedmontese peppers 66
Periwinkles: Oyster and onion tart 87
Persillade: Roast leg of lamb with persillade 14
Pheasant: Braised pheasant with cream and pimenton 127
Pimenton: Braised pheasant with cream and pimenton 127
Pineapple: Grilled pineapple with chilli syrup and coconut ice cream 102
Polenta 101

Pork
Breast of veal with pork, spinach and garlic stuffing 55
Le Cassoulet 133
Roast grouse 89
Roast loin of pork with herbs and garlic 73
Potatoes 38
Aligot 40
Basic mash 38
Champ 39
Cream of fennel soup with tapenade croutons 112
Crème Palestine 151
New potatoes in milk 40
Parsnip, Jerusalem artichoke, celeriac or swede mash 40
Potato and cep cake 94
Potato, fennel and rosemary risotto 79
Quick roast potatoes with onions, garlic and rosemary 41
Red mullet, aubergine and potato sandwich 61
Roast garlic mash 40
Saffron and olive oil mash 39
Prawn biryani 80
Pumpkin soup with cream and Gruyère 105

Quinces: Baked quinces with cinnamon and Vin Santo 129

Raspberries
Baked tamarillos with vanilla ice cream 31
Raspberry gratin 62
Sauternes and olive oil cake with red fruit salad 56
Summer pudding 69
Red mullet, aubergine and potato sandwich 61
Redcurrants
Sauternes and olive oil cake with red fruit salad 56
Summer pudding 69
Rhubarb 27
Rhubarb fool 22
John Dory with rhubarb 25
Rice 77
Courgette and gorgonzola risotto 78
Pilaff 79
Potato, fennel and rosemary risotto 79
Prawn biryani 80
Pumpkin soup with cream and Gruyère 105
Risotto milaneses 77
Risotto primavera 78
Wild mushroom risotto 93

Rosemary
Potato, fennel and rosemary risotto 79
Quick roast potatoes with onions, garlic and
rosemary 41

Saffron and olive oil mash 39
Sage: Red onions with sage and lemon 49
Salads
Crab and papaya salad 29
Escarole, pear and Roquefort salad 98
Greek salad 73
Salade Niçoise 54, 57
Sauternes and olive oil cake with red fruit salad 56
Salmon: Raw salmon with ginger dressing 34
Salsify 128
Sauces
Bagna cauda sauce 50
Bread sauce 89
Cod with parsley sauce139
Coffee bean sauce 17
Cumberland sauce 146
Sauternes and olive oil cake with red fruit salad 56
Scallops: Griddled scallops with pea purée and mint
vinaigrette 126, 130
Sea kale with blood orange hollandaise 21
Shallots
Bagna cauda sauce 50
Skirt steak with shallots 30
Shrimp paste 144
Skirt steak with shallots 30
Soups
Chilled avocado and almond soup 60
Cream of chicken and mushroom soup 13
Cream of fennel soup with tapenade croutons 112
Mussel soup 138
Pumpkin soup with cream and Gruyère 105
Spinach
Breast of veal with pork, spinach and garlic stuffing 55
Spiced spinach 114
Strawberries
Sauternes and olive oil cake with red fruit salad 56
Wild strawberry pudding 36
Swede mash 40

Tamarillos: Baked tamarillos with vanilla ice cream 31
Tapenade: Cream of fennel soup with tapenade
croutons 112
Tarragon: Roast chicken with tarragon 67

Tomatoes
Fettuccine with mussels 116
Greek salad 73
Grilled tomatoes and fennel with basil 50
Imam Bayildi 113
Salade Niçoise 54, 57
Tian of tomatoes and aubergines 68
Tuna and cherry tomato brochette with salmoriglio 48
Trout: Sea trout fillet with a horseradish crust 21
Tuna and cherry tomato brochette with salmoriglio 48
Turnip gratin 15

Veal: Breast of veal with pork, spinach and garlic
stuffing 55
Venison stew with baby onions, chestnuts and
chocolate 99
Vin Santo
Baked quinces with cinnamon and Vin Santo 129
Biscotti and Vin Santo ice cream 153

Wine 159
Baked quinces with cinnamon and Vin Santo 129
Biscotti and Vin Santo ice cream 153
Poached pears in Beaujolais 95
Sauternes and olive oil cake with red fruit salad 56